P.S. Joseph 2 J

Phil 4:19

THE UNKNOWN SOLDIERS

Black Missionaries of the 20th Century

Author: Reverend Dr. Joseph C. Jeter Sr.

Have Christ Will Travel Ministries

Philadelphia, Pennsylvania

Date Written: September 7, 1998 – February 9, 2003

Copyright © 2004 by Dr. Joseph C. Jeter

ISBN 0-7414-2062-7

Published by:

INFINITY
PUBLISHING.COM

1094 New Dehaven Street, Suite 100
West Conshohocken, PA 19428-2713
Info@buybooksontheweb.com
www.buybooksontheweb.com
Toll-free (877) BUY BOOK
Local Phone (610) 941-9999
Fax (610) 941-9959

Printed in the United States of America

Printed on Recycled Paper

Published July 2004

Table of Contents

FOREWORD

This book is dedicated to people like Mother Winnie Mae Lane, (Christ Baptist Church, Philadelphia, Pennsylvania), who serve on both home and foreign mission fields and has never received recognition or acknowledgement as a missionary. The same can also be said for missionary, Bonnie Starkey Bazemore, (Have Christ Will Travel Ministries) who has served as a missionary, office manager, counselor, and has done general mission work for more than 18 years. (As of the date of this Foreword, February 19, 2003, Bonnie Starkey Bazemore's ministry is ongoing.) This saint in many circles is not considered a missionary. Missionary Bonnie Bazemore is from Evergreen Baptist Christ, Washington, D.C., (Reverend Robert King is the Pastor and is fruit from the late Dr. Reverend Herman Connoly, Berean Bible Baptist Church, Altanta, Georgia.)

I also dedicate this book to my wife Catherine E. Jeter and my children Diane M. Jeter, Dr. Rhonda F. Jeter, Joseph C. Jeter, Jr., Priscilla R. Jeter Iles, and Major Paul E. Jeter, Esquire, United States Air Force.

I also dedicate this book to the many unknown Black American missionaries, who served the Lord Jesus Christ in world missions in the late 19th and 20th centuries. I have not listed all of them. Many have been left out of this book not because they are less, but my time to do research is short. The missionaries that are listed, I may have had personal contact with. If any person is offended because they are not listed, please forgive me.

In Hebrews Chapter 11, there is a roll call of the Heroes of the Faith, and their deeds done in the name of our Lord Jesus. All these are known because they are written in scripture. These people did many of the same deeds; many of them suffered by faith, labored by faith, endured afflictions by faith, etc. and are well known by the Godhead in heaven but not by men. They are the unknown soldiers of God in the 19th and 20th centuries. Black, Colored, Negro, African American, and whatever else you will call them, missionaries sent by the Lord, used by the Lord, they finished their work, but unlike the people in Hebrews Chapter 11 they are unknown, rejected almost by the church. They received the promise of God and have finished their course or are in the midst of it. "So Send I you," by E. Margaret Clarkson, 1915; and the music by John W. Peterson, 1921:

"So send I you to labor unrewarded,
To serve unpaid, unloved, unsought, unknown,
To bear rebuke to suffer scorn and scoffing,
So send I you to toil for Me alone.

So send I you to bind the bruise and broken,
O'er wondering souls to work, to weep, to wake.
To bear the burdens of a world aweary,
So send I you to suffer for My sake.

So send I you to loneliness and longing
With heart ahungring for the loved and known,
Forsaking home and kindred, friend and dear one,
So send I you to know My love alone.

So send I you to leave your life's ambition,
To die to dear desire, self-will resign,
To labor long and love where me revile you.
So send I you to lose your life in Mine.

So send I you to hearts made hard by hatred,
To eyes made blind because they will not see,
To spend tho' it be blood to spend and spare not,
So send I you to taste of Calvary.

As the Father has sent me, So send I you."

COMMENTS

As I reviewed the notes on the Unknown Soldier by Dr. Joseph C. Jeter Sr., I feel that there is a wealth of information that can be encouraging and informative to many people. Many who may read this book will follow the steps of these Heroes of the Faith in Jesus Christ. Their life commitment and experience unto the Lord Jesus Christ is outstanding.

These blessed accounts of Black missionaries truly are a legacy to be remembered and a model to the glory of God. "Therefore, my beloved brethren, be steadfast, immovable, always abounding in the work of the Lord, knowing that your labor is not in the vain in the Lord."

I Corinthians 15:58

Missionary Catherine E. Jeter

PROLOGUE

The Unknown Soldier

This is a factual record of missions. Black missionaries, who served on foreign and home mission fields; in America and on different foreign fields around the world. Most of these saints of God are not known. The church does not know them, our nation does not know them, Black culture does not know them, and there is very little documentation of their works. These wonderful people have served and risked their lives for the cause of the gospel of our Lord Jesus Christ. They are known in heaven but not known on earth. They have gone and given the good news of salvation, through grace, through faith plus nothing. "So Send I You," hymnbook "Great Hymns of Faith," by E. Margaret Clarkson, 1915; and the music by John W. Peterson, 1921:

"So send I you to labor unrewarded,
To serve unpaid, unloved, unsought, unknown,
To bear rebuke to suffer scorn and scoffing,
So send I you to toil for Me alone.

So send I you to bind the bruised and broken,
O'er wondering souls to work, to weep, to wake.
To bear the burdens of a world aweary,
So send I you to suffer for My sake.

So send I you to loneliness and longing
With heart ahungring for the loved and known,
Forsaking home and kindred, friend and dear one,
So send I you to know My love alone.

So send I you to leave your life's ambition,
To die to dear desire, self-will resign,
To labor long and love where men revile you.
So send I you to lose your life in Mine.

So send I you to hearts made hard by hatred,
To eyes made blind because they will not see,
To spend tho' it be blood to spend and spare not,
So send I you to taste of Calvary.

As the Father has sent me, So send I you."

My name is Dr. Joseph C. Jeter, Sr. My wife Catherine E. Jeter and I have served on home and foreign fields as missionaries for 39 years. This is not my story but as much as I am able to remember, the story of unknown soldiers. I do not know all of them, some I have forgotten etc., but as they are remembered, or someone brings them to my attention, they will be added.

ROLL CALL

Missionary #1 Mother Eliza Davis George

Mother Eliza Davis George, began her ministry with the National Baptist Convention USA in 1911, and served with that organization until 1917 at the Suen Mission, Liberia West Africa. Her mission continued in Liberia West Africa from 1918-1949. Her ministry was with the National Baptist Convention of America in Greenville Sinoe County, Liberia, West Africa. From 1949-1973 she founded and labored with the Evangelical Negro Industrial Mission, Sinoe County, Liberia. Mother George died in 1979 or 1980 in Taylor, Texas at the age of 100 years old. Her ministry was church and school planting, evangelism, child development, Christian education, etc. Probably, Eliza Davis George is the greatest Black American missionary in modern time. I met Mother George at the ENI Mission deep in the bush at the age of 91. Her ministry was vast. At the time that I met her in the 1970s, she was at the ENI Mission building a child development center. She was almost blind, she walked with a walking stick, she had a large tropical ulcer on her leg, and she was still pressing the claims of Christ. It was a great honor to have met and fellowshiped with her.

Missionary #2 Reverend Montrose Waite

Reverend Montrose Waite began his missionary work with the Christian and Missionary Alliance in 1923 and remained there until 1938. He served in Sierra Leone and Guinea, West Africa. In 1949, he founded the Afro-American Missionary Crusade. The Afro-American Missionary Crusade is the first Black faith mission in the United States. Under this organization Reverend Waite founded the Bopolu Bible Mission, Liberia, West Africa. Reverend Waite along with *Reverend Dr. Ernest L. Wilson* was an inspiration to many young people in the Philadelphia area and encouraged them to become full-time faith missionaries. *Dorothy Evans, Mother Martha Thompson,* and I are sure he was an inspiration for people like *Virginia Antrom,* National Baptist Convention USA, Philadelphia, Pennsylvania. Reverend Waite's ministry with the Afro-American Missionary Crusade was from 1948-1961 He then went to Atlanta, Georgia and met *Reverend Talmage Payne (a white minister)* and they founded the second Black faith mission board Carver Foreign Missions. The Afro-American Missionary Crusade and the Carver Foreign Missions were both sending boards. *Sister Naomi Doyle* and *Sister Cora McCleary,* were the first two missionaries sent to Liberia West Africa by Carver Foreign Missions. Many missionaries followed: *Mary Stephens, Mable McComb* (Mary Stephens was Baptist, Mable McComb was AME), *Sister Henrietta Herron,* and *Reverend Donald and Charlotte Canty.* Many others such as *Reverend* and *Mrs. Bryant Johnson,* and *Reverend and Mrs. Glenn Mason* etc., followed Reverend Waite's ministry with Carver Foreign Missions which was from about 1958-1973. On his last trip to West Africa at the approximate age of 80 years old, he went from mission to mission making repairs, preaching, and teaching the gospel. He even built a mud oven to bake bread, at the Salala Mission in Liberia West Africa. Mother *Edith Johnson* was overjoyed. Reverend Waite also did administration and building. He did village evangelism all over Liberia. He made one more trip to East Africa the country of Tanzenia with the revival church of East Africa just before or near the end of his life.

Missionary #3 Mother Edith Johnson (United Holy Church of America)

Mother Edith Johnson also trained young missionaries from other missions. She loved to trek and preach in the bush. Mother Johnson was also involved with child development, evangelism and church planning. She educated many children and saw many come to Christ. Like many Black missionaries, she was forgotten by her denomination, sometimes getting funds once or twice a year, as the mission offerings in the Black church in the United States of America were pennies. (Today it is still a very small offering in the church.) Mother Johnson had two people who stuck with her on the field, one was a Liberian sister whose name was *Malverna Harris* she was faithful, the other was *Reverend Sister Ella Carrol*. Sister Carrol was an independent faith missionary who was called by God to be with Mother Johnson. Because she was not a part of Mother Johnson's denomination she got money regularly and helped support the work, she had a better car etc. Let it be said that the early Black missionaries whether faith missionaries or denominational, put all their money into their work. The newer missionaries seem to want to take all that they can from the work. (This statement may not be true, but I place it in here for a reflection.) Mother Edith Johnson did a great deal more than these few lines can tell. Through her musical talent she was able to reach into the country of Liberia by radio. She spoke with Liberian Presidents Tubman and Talbert. She sang at councils and conferences at home and abroad. She was a tough, sweet, hard nosed lady, totally committed to the Lord Jesus Christ. She was holy and one of the great Black missionaries of modern time.

Mother Johnson did a great, great many things but one of the greatest feats was when she built her own mission house because there were not enough American men missionaries in Salala, Liberia. Mother Johnson built a mud block house, she put in aluminum-framed windows and got up on the roof and nailed the roof on herself. She was not the only Black American missionary woman to do things like that. She was outstanding in leading the way and whatever she could do to enhance her ministry and minister the gospel, she did it. There is much more to be said about Mother Johnson. Someone else will probably do a better job than I have in describing her, but let me tell you one thing, she was a preacher, she was a teacher, she was a worker and she's now resting from her labors in Glory. Her work follows her. Edith Johnson, a great Black missionary of the 20th century. How we praise the Lord for her.

I would imagine that Mother Johnson's work started in the late 1940's and continued until her death sometime in the mid-1990's. Her work, I want to reiterate, crossed denominational lines as people loved her and ministered to her so that she could do mission work. *Reverened Herman Connoly* of Berean Bible Baptist Church of Atlanta, Georgia was a great lover of Edith Johnson's work and visited and supported her work in Liberia. Reverend Robert King of Evergreen Baptist Church, Washington, DC also loved her and ministered much to her work.[1]

Missionary #4 Mother August Tyler

August Tyler was the founder of the Voice of Africa Mission in 1963 or 1964. Mother Tyler was from Oakland, California and a member of the North Oakland Baptist Church. Mother Tyler moved to Bassa Geah Town in Grand Bassa County Liberia, West Africa in 1967. She was a graduate of the Bay Cities Bible Institute, Oakland California. Mother Tyler probably got her missionary burden from the life of *Mother Eliza Davis* George, the greatest Black missionary of modern times. Because Mother Tyler's roots were in Texas, where Mother George came from, around 1911, Mother Tyler had a burden for the lost in Africa. After completing Bay Cities Bible Institution in Oakland, California, she founded the Voice of Africa Mission and incorporated it in the State of California. From what I can tell, after seeking workers to go to the field in Liberia, West Africa and finding none, she sold all she owned and (she made contact with another old missionary named Mother Holmes of the New York City, New York who had worked in Liberia) she focused on Liberia. She also made contact

---

[1] Reverend Dr. Herman Connoly, Berean Bible Baptist Christ, Atlanta George was also the Deputation Secretary for Carver Foreign Missions.

with Sister Grazelle Settles of New Bethlehem Baptist Church, Philadelphia, Pennsylvania; Manna Bible Institute, Philadelphia, Pennsylvania; also a graduate of Praire Bible Institute in Three Hills Alberta in Canada. Praire Bible Institute was a great faith school, August Tyler asked Sister Settles to go to Liberia with her. Grazelle Settles agreed and they went to Liberia and started to work at the mission that Mother Holmes had started. With the death of Mother Holmes and not being able to get the deeds to the land that constituted a tribal grant (Zordee Mission), Mother Tyler and Mother Settles looked for another area for the Voice of Africa to develop viable work. Mother Holmes' work was near the road junction of the Town of Clay, nine to 15 miles from Monrovia and about a three hour walk to the west of the road gate at Clay; six to eight miles in the deep bush with only a little pathway or trail.

As the two missionaries prayed, Chief Bassa Geah sent for them to come to Grand Bassa County to Bassa Geah Town. He offered Mother Tyler a tribal grant of between 150 and 500 acres of land to build a mission school, a church and to start an agricultural project near Bassa Geah Town. Mother Tyler and Mother Settles agreed, and moved from the mission near Clay in Loffa County, almost 200 miles away to Bassa Geah Town and began to build a Voice of Africa Mission campus on the site they were given. They brought some of the children that they had been training at Mother Holmes' mission and soon they had at least 75 children at the Voice of Africa Mission for training. They began with ABC's and went through the sixth grade. The children were older children and some younger ones, even a little older children; 9-15 years old. She had 75 children there for training. I first found these two great ladies on my first missionary trip to Liberia, West Africa in 1966. By the time I returned in March of 1967, they were at the new mission in Bassa Geah Town 200 miles from Monrovia. What was Augusta Tyler's vision?: 1) to take the gospel to Africa, 2) to prove that Black Christians could found, operate and produce in faith missions; 3) to build a Christian high school deep in the bush; and 4) to foster the total Christian education experience concept for tribal people outside of the metropolitan area in Liberia. This has been done before by denominational churches: National Baptist Convention USA, United Holy Church of American, and possibly the Church of the Living God headquartered in Philadelphia, Bishop White in the 1960s. The concept developed from the United Pentecostal Council of the Assemblies of God Cambridge, Massachusetts and Christ of God in Christ in America. This was the first attempt to do this by a Black leadership faith mission. There were many others that I do not know of but I think this was the first. It may be the second with the Bopolu Bible Mission being first. Though she did not get her high school built, she did a great job in ministering from K-8th grade. Her failure to complete the high school building was because of the lack of vision of her supporters to help her; there was no money. Mother Tyler may not have had a college education, but she had a vision and she worked on it for 38 to 42 years. She died on March 19, 1998, still pressing toward the mark of her vision and calling at 91 years of age. At the time of this writing, February 19, 2003, the Voice of Africa Mission is semi-dormant. Some of the children that she raised were able to reach America and pursued their education. At this time, some of them are trying to revive the mission.

Missionary #5 Mother Emma B. Delaney

Early Black Missionary Emma B. Delaney, National Baptist Convention USA. Emma B. DeLaney's ministry is from 1900-1905 in Nyasaland, East Africa, which is now the country of Malawi. Sister Delaney worked for six years in Malawi or Nyasaland. Nyasaland/Malawi is landlocked, so she walked 200 miles from the Indian Ocean to what is now Blantyre Malawi. Because of her ministry, there is a huge mission at Churad Zulu Malawi about 10 or 15 miles outside of Blantyre. At the time of her ministry, probably the town of Blantyre was named Liverstone or Livingstonia after the great Missionary Robert Livingstone who went into Africa and explored.   Mother Delaney had a great ministry apparently preaching, teaching, and evangelism etc.   She stayed there six years 1900-1905 and left, never to return to East Africa.   She does appear at Suen Mission in Liberia West   Africa   around   1909.   From   her   work   in Nyasaland/Malawi, there must be many churches and over 150,000 people were converted in Malawi, Congo, Zaire, and Tanzania from her ministry.   Much more can be said about her work, but more research is needed.   She is a great pioneer in foreign missions who has had a great impact on East and West Africa as a Black missionary.

Fruit from her ministry is *Dr. Daniel S. Malekebu* a leader for many years on the field of Malawi East Africa.[2]   I, Dr. Joseph C. Jeter founder of Have Christ Will Travel Ministries, made two visits to that field in 1970 and 1971. I found a great work there.

Missionary #6 Mother Viola Reddish

Mother Viola Reddish, she was with Lott Cary Mission and the Afro-American Missionary Crusades.[3]   Her last work was at the Bopolu Bible Mission, Bopolu Liberia West Africa.   The Afro-American Missionary Crusade is the first Black leadership faith mission in America.   Mother Viola Reddish was a great missionary.   She was very energetic and a woman of vision, and she had a great burden for Africa.   I met Mother Viola Reddish in Philadelphia, Pennsylvania in

---

[2] Dr. Daniel S. Malekebu, National Baptist ConventionUSA Headquarters, Churad Zulu Town, about fifteen miles outside of Blantyre Malawi.

[3] Mother Viola Reddish is from North Penn Baptist Church located at 27nd and Hagert Street in the village section of Philadelphia, Pennsylvania. She is a great, great missionary. She is a graduate of Virginia Union University and she was a missionary with the Lott Cary Convention in the 1950s. She got sick and was sent home and later joined the Afro-American Mission Crusades.

the fall of 1961 or 1962. She was home on furlough after three or four years of hard labor at Bopolu Bible Mission. The mission station was about 60 miles deep in the bush in Loffa County, Liberia. I believe the tribe she was working with was the Kppelle Tribe. Her duties were many; teacher in the mission school and principle sometimes, preacher at the Bopolu Bible Church, preacher at the mission preaching stations at Loma, Totaqule, Soplama, Vongana, Fosweta and other towns that she visited as she ministered the gospel. She walked many hours each week to these bush villages with poor food and very little rest. Eventually her body broke down. Viola was committed to the Lord Jesus Christ and was a the Lott Cary Mission between 9-15 miles outside of Monrovia Liberia, before she went to the Bopolu Bible Mission; she was teaching school and ministering the Word of God there. She got sick from malaria and from a disease called falaria and was sent home by the *Lott Cary* Mission. The time she spent with the Lott Cary Mission, I do not know, but in 1961 she was home on furlough from the Bopolu Bible Mission so, she must have been there from 1954-1955. She must have begun her service with the Afro-American Missionary Crusade around 1957 or 1958. Mother Reddish must have met Reverend Montrose Waite and he urged her to come to Bopolu. Viola Reddish served valiantly along with Martha Thompson, and Dorothy Evans. They made up the Philadelphia arm of the missionary force at Bopolu Bible Mission. Mother Reddish had problems with filarial and malaria. Her health broken down in 1970 or 1971 and she died in the Elwa Hospital in July 1970 or 1971 in Painesville, Liberia.

Mother Reddish led many to Christ. She was a blessing to many. Her burden for Africa and her dedication to the cause of missions, and the gospel, and the Lord Jesus Christ will live forever in the hearts of those who knew her. Her mission ministry is 11 ½ to 20 years. She was a member for a little while of my church, Marston Temple Baptist Church, Philadelphia, Pa. She was active there until she returned to the field to die. She was an inspiration to my wife, my family and I, as she tried to stir us up for a vision in the world missions. Viola Reddish missionary supreme and her works do follow her.

Missionary #7 Mother Vera Stephen

Mother Vera Stephen, Chicago Illinois. Vera Stephen is from the United Pentecostal Council of the Assemblies of God (UPC) in Cambridge, MA. Vera Stephen was a magnificent missionary. Mother Stephen's foreign missionary work began as a UPC missionary in Yarmouth, Nova Scotia in the 1950s. How long she ministered at Sharon Gospel Assembly in the south end area of Yarmouth I do not know. She was able to influence the late *Reverend Prince Albert Best* of Cambridge, MA to take her her place in Yarmouth, Nova Scotia in Atlantic Canada when she went to Liberia, West Africa under Child Evangelism Fellowship. She did great work in children's ministry for over 31 years. She trained and sent African workers all over Liberia to do child evangelism. She endured the hardship of missionary life in West Africa as she had a vision and burden to transmit across Liberia, West Africa the Gospel of Jesus Christ. *Vera Stephen* was one of the first senior missionaries to receive short-term missionaries from Have Christ Will Travel Ministries. Mother Stephen continued to expand her ministry near the Painsville area 15 miles from Monrovia. She built a camp, a church, and a boarding school for Liberian young people from K-8th grade. Mother Stephens planted a church in an area that was caught up in the Civil War in Liberia. As she protected her children, age and hardship took its toll upon her. She became sick in 1993 or 1994 and died. She was buried on her school and camp grounds in Liberia West Africa in Painsville about 12-15 miles from Monrovia. She leaves an indelible mark because of her ministry and commitment to world missions and child evangelism. Mother Vera Stephens' ministry must have spanned 40 years. I don't know what age she was when she died, but she was on fire for the Lord.

Missionary #8 Mother Anita Bolden Fitts

Missionary Anita Bolden Fitts, Pittsburgh, Pennsylvania. Mother Fitts until a few years ago in 1995 was the oldest living Black American missionary in the United State in the 1990s. She was 99 years old at her home going. Mother Fitts was a graduate of Nyack Bible College somewhere around 1920 in Nyack, New York.

She received her missionary call at an early age in Pittsburgh, Pennsylvania probably at the Colored Christian and Missionary Alliance Church in the Hill District of Pittsburgh, PA. She received the call at the church she attended. She finished her training at Nyack Bible College and became a missionary under the Christian and Missionary Alliance Mission board to West Africa.

Her ministry began in Guinea West Africa and in Sierra Leone. She did general mission work: preaching, teaching, church planning, and Bible translation. She also formatted a hymnbook from English into the Koronco language. Her Bible translation work was great. Mother Fitts is probably the first Black American Christian on record to do this type of work, translating the scripture portions from English to the Koronco language. Mother Fitts worked in very primitive bush conditions. I think she was a missionary from 1922-1929 or 1930. Mother Fitts worked in primitive bush conditions deep into the areas of Guinea and Sierra Leone, by train and foot walking many miles, and sleeping in mud huts nightly under a mosquito net.

Her ministry in West Africa lasted for seven years 1923-1929. She did a valiant job. Many souls were saved, churches planted and the Lord Jesus Christ was glorified. When she returned home in 1929 she did not return to the field, but she prayed, she ministered, she projected the mission enterprise in the Black church for the balance of her life. She was also a member of the Salvation Army for many years. Mother Fitts was a holy woman of God. Two Black American missionary men who served with her in the same country were Reverend Montrose Waite, Cleveland, Ohio and Reverend Eugene Thornly of Philadelphia, Pennsylvania.

Missionary #9 Mother Maddie Lee Monroe

Maddie Lee Monroe was a member of the Berkley Mt. Zion Baptist Church, Berkley California. Mother Monroe is also the founder of the Evangelical Negro Industrial Mission Incorporated (ENI) in Oakland, California. This mission was founded to support Mother Eliza Davis George's ENI Mission in the Sinoe County area of Liberia. It was founded around 1949 or 1950 when Mother George broke away from the National Baptist Convention of America, because she had retired by that time.

The ENI Mission that Mother Monroe founded gave the prayer and financial support that was needed as Mother George had started a faith mission to continue her work of church planting, child evangelism and child development after she was forced to retire by the National Baptist Convention of America around the age of 72. The second goal of Mother Monroe was to work in home missions giving the gospel to the lost in the Greater Oakland area. Mother Monroe had a care group of sisters who worked with her and ministered with her; *Sister Edna B. Moody, Sister Haillie Q. Smith, Sister Allie James, Sister Morell Posey* and many others carried on the work.

Around 1969, Mother Monroe was moved by God to make a world tour. While she was on this tour her husband died. While on the tour God spoke to her to return home and she put Edna Moody and Hallie Q. Smith in charge of the work and return to Sinoe County, Liberia to work at the ENI Mission. Her work was elementary education and Bible;

preaching and teaching in the villages where Mother George had established work.

Mother Monroe suffered much in her 3-5 year ministry in Africa. In 1970, I found her in the field in horrible condition while ministering to the glory of God. I returned in 1971 to find both her and Mother George in the mist of building a child development center deep in the bush. Mother Monroe was faithful to here calling in 1974 or 1975, but she returned to Oakland, California never to return to the foreign field. Her physical and mental health was broken, but the victory was in the completion of the purpose. At the time of this writing, September 17, 1998, Mother Maddie Lee Monroe lived in a group home in Oakland, California at the age of 80-82 years old. The price she paid was high. The ENI Mission remains at 3140 Union Street, Oakland, California. Missionary *Thessa McCoy* is the President, *Morell Posie* and *Allie James* are still active along with Annie Lee Ervin of Oakland, California doing the work that the ENI Mission was called to do. Since the time of this writing, Annie Lee Ervin is with the Lord, Maddie Lee Monroe is with the Lord, and Allie James is still with us at the time of this writing in February 2003 and the work is going on. Maddie Lee Monroe. "Also now, behold, my witness is in heaven, and my record on high," Job 16:19.

Missionary #10 Reverend Bob Harrison

Reverend Harrison is still alive at the time of the writing of this book; he must be about 80 years old. Reverend Harrison is a great missionary; he is a preacher, singer and Bible teacher. Reverend Harrison is an international evangelist and missionary. He is from the Assemblies of God Church. He has worked with *Reverend Billy Graham* and the Billy Graham team in crusades around the world. Reverend Harrison is the most notable Black Christian from the Assemblies of God Church in America and was as far as I can tell the first Black missionary to work with OC

Ministries as a full-time missionary in the Philippians and Southeast Asia. Reverend Harrison's ministry opened the door for many Black missionaries to work with white mission boards. Reverend Harrison's ministry has been in place for more than 45 years. In the later years, Reverend Bob Harrison formed the Bob Harrison's Ministries, an international evangelistic ministry that runs crusades all over the world. Bob's focus is on evangelism, soul winning and discipleship. His crusades in Africa and Asia have been a great success. Reverend Harrison is also an author having written many books and is a giant in the world on the world mission scene. Revered Bob is better known in the white Christian world than in the Black Christian world. I say this to qualify Reverend Harrison as an unknown Soldier. I would again assert that Reverend Bob Harrison has made a great impact on world missions.

Reverend Bob Harrison's son is now a missionary in South Africa. Reverend Bob Harrison, Sr. lives in the San Francisco Bay Area today and is open to preach and teach the gospel worldwide. Bob's ministry must span from the middle 1950s into the year 2003. Bob Harrison sacrificial lamb for the spread of the gospel around the world, may the Lord bless him and keep him. At the time of the writing of this book February 19, 2003, Bob is still alive.

Missionary #11 Mother Erma Bailey Ethridge

Erma Bailey Ethridge is a tremendous missionary from a church where I was converted in Philadelphia called the Wayland Temple Baptist Church. If I am not mistaken, Erma Bailey Ethridge is a graduate of Virginia Union University and she is a great woman. Erma was born in Philadelphia, Pennsylvania. Sister Erma was from Wayland Temple Baptist Church in North Philadelphia. She was a missionary to Liberia West Africa under the National Baptist Convention USA. She went out from the Wayland Temple

Baptist Church when Reverend C.M. Smith was the pastor in the 1950s. Erma went to the mission field about the same time that I went out to serve in the Korean War in the early 1950s. She ministered in Liberia for over 40 years. Her ministry was teaching Bible and secular education at the Suen Mission. She also taught at the Baptist Mission located at the Cape Mount and at the Outreach Station National Baptist Convention USA near #1 Gate in Grand Bassa County, deep down in the bush in Liberia. She may have preached and taught Sunday School etc. Her ministry was mostly in the bush on mission stations. For a while after she married a Liberian brother, she labored at a home for children in an area in Liberia called Virginia. The Sunday School at Wayland Temple Church under the leadership of *Mother Lotie Churn* supported Mother Erma Bailey Ethridge faithfully for 40 years. Mother Ehtridge was faithful at her post at Suen Mission when the revolution under Charles Taylor broke out in 1990 or 1991. She remained in Liberia when all the American missionaries were evacuated in 1993. Because she had Liberian citizenship, she suffered many things during the war and suffered mental abuse as Suen was taken over by one of the fighting factions. After many problems Mother Ethridge was able to return to America. Her health broken and her mental state stricken, she continued to serve the Lord. After a long illness she went to be with the Lord in 1994 in Richmond, Virginia. The late Janice Elliott from Philadelphia, labored much to get Sister Elthridge here to America and then to help her get much needed medical treatment and was deeply involved with Mother Ethridge. At the time of her home going all of us were sadden and yet rejoicing. Servant of God well done the battle fought, the victory won, enter into the joy of the Lord. "I have fought a good fight, I have finished my course, I have kept the faith," II Timothy 4:7.

Missionary #12 Mother Maggie Lampkin

Mother Maggie Lampkin of Oakland, California served in Liberia, West Africa. How many years she served is not clear to me, but Mother Lampkin was there when I arrived on the mission scene in March 1966 and as the Liberians would say, "she had been there ever since." She went to the field under the Soul Clinic Mission or Church in the Home Mission out of Los Angeles, California with *Fred Jordan*. She was a member of, as much as I can determine, a Baptist church in Oakland, California. I would imagine that the time of her ministry may have been 1955-1970 somewhere during this time frame.

Her mission was known as the Soul Clinic Mission near Parker Paint about 15 miles outside of Monrovia Liberia and about a mile off the Monrovia Kakata Road in the bush. Her work was soul winning, evangelism, church planting, preaching, child development and Christian education. She had a Christian boarding school for girls, and she may have had boys also. The Church in the Home Mission is a faith mission "white leadership". Her ministry must have begun in the 1950s. She was probably one of the few Black missionaries at that time with a white mission board. Reverend Bob Harrison, from the San Francisco Bay Area with OC ministries, may have been another.

Maggie Lampkin's work may have inspired other Black missionaries from the Oakland California area. Maggie Lampkin was a holy lady, tough as steel, filled with the Holy Spirit and on the move for God. She also had a vision to reproduce Black missionaries, and took some of the early Black faith short-term missionaries from Have Christ Will Travel in the early 1970s. Maggie Lampkin suffered much from minimal support. She suffered much from the pressures of faith living both physical and the hard bush conditions. Even after she was diagnosed with Cancer, she continued her ministry until she was near death before she returned to America to take off to heaven. In the late 1970s or early 1980s, the Church in the Home Mission had another mission station deep in the bush in Grand Bassa County near Compound 3. A couple is remembered in this article because they were teammates with Mother Lampkin. Their first names I do not know, but they were always referred to as the Ottoes, Ma and Pa Otto. The Church in the Home missionaries loved each other; because of this love I was able to stop and be refreshed as I traveled to minister on different missions and to missionaries. Maggie Lampkin will always be remembered in Black mission history as a steadfast giant for the Lord Jesus Christ. "I press toward the mark for the prize of the high calling of God in Christ Jesus," Philippians 3:14.

Missionary #13 Dr. Ernest L. Wilson

Dr. Ernest L. Wilson, Philadelphia, Pennsylvania, New Bethlehem Baptist Church at Preston and Aspen Street, Philadelphia, Pennsylvania. Dr. Ernest L. Wilson is a co-founder of the Afro-American Missionary Crusade. It was the first Black leadership faith mission established in America in 1949. Reverend Wilson was a world Christian with ministries in Panama and Central America and was an inspiration to the Black Christian community for youth ministries. He is also the first one to call for faith promise giving in the Black church, in the United States.

Through the inspiration of Dr. Wilson, young people like Dorothy Evans and Martha Thompson became foreign missionaries. He probably had an influence on men like Tom Skinner etc. More can be learned about Dr. Wilson in the Dr. Ernest L. Wilson's story by Dr. Joseph C. Jeter, Philadelphia, Pennsylvania. He was a world traveler. He was the one who got me interested in world missions. He invited me to Uganda in East Africa in 1964, and I ventured to Uganda in 1965. Through his influence I met *Harry Campbell* of Uganda Book Shops, *Corrie Ten Boom* and *Roy Hesson,* the Author of Calvary Road. Roy Hesson and Harry

Campbell were from the East African Revival movement from 1960 – 1972. Things began to happen. A little booklet will be put out about Dr. Ernest L. Wilson soon.

Missionary #14 Sister Naomi Doles Mitchell

Missionary Naomi Doles Mitchell, Carver Foreign Missions. Naomi Doles Mitchell was a young missionary candidate from Portsmouth, Virginia. She was a student at Carver Bible College in Atlanta, Georgia and had a missionary call on her life.[4] She may have come into contact with Reverend Montrose Waite on one of his deputation trips into Virginia, Georgia or Mississippi. She also may have come into contact with him at the Carver Bible College. Sister Doles with the completion of her Bible training became the first candidate of Carver Foreign Missions somewhere between 1959 and 1961.

At the time of her mission commitment to Carver Missions, so I am told, she was suppose to marry the Reverend Luther Mitchell. I have been told *Reverend Luther Mitchell* did not meet the education requirements to be a candidate with Carver Foreign Missions. Naomi's call and commitment to the Lord Jesus Christ was so deep that the wedding was postponed as the call of God took precedence over everything else. Naomi Doles and *Mother Cora McCleary* were the first two missionaries sent out by Carver Foreign Missions to establish the Monrovia Bible Institute and also to start a school in King Gray Village, which is now the Carver Christian Academy. Since these two great ladies had no field experience, they were sent to Mother Edith Johnson at

---

[4] Special attention must be given to Naomi Doles Mitchell. The first part will deal with Naomi Doles Mitchell, Carver Foreign Mission, King Gray Village, Painsville, Liberia and the Monrovia Bible Institute on Benson Street in Monrovia, Liberia. The second part will deal with Naomi Doles Mitchell and Reverend Luther Mitchell in Sinoe County, Liberia at the Bessmen Town Mission Station, Church of Christ Holiness and the last year of Luther Mitchell, Church of Christ Holiness as he rebuilt the mission house, Monrovia, Liberia West Africa.

the Salala Mission to get field training before they went to King Gray Village and into Monrovia, Liberia to establish a Bible Institute. Naomi Doles was not a very large lady, but she was full of fire and had a great sense of mission. The suffering and sacrifice that was needed to establish Carver Christian Academy and the Monrovia Bible Institute was great! There was not much equipment and the weather was harsh in the rainy season. The weather took its toll, but Sister Doles pressed forward. There were so few Black men in missions at the time, so men like *Revered Ernest Wilson*, *Reverend Ben Johnson* and I were rare. I made visits to the Carver Mission Compound near King Gray Village.

I saw the hard work in the village grade school. A pre-primer through 6 grade school was established at King Gray Village. In 1966, just before leaving Liberia to return to America, Sister Doles, *Sister Mary Stevens* and *Sister Cora McCleary* pleaded with me to find a man to come to the field to help them with the church they had planted in King Gray Village, as well as to lead the Bible institute. I was very moved by the efforts of these ladies. I do not know how they were able to endure the hardships and labor so valiantly. Upon my return to America, I made the need known, and *Reverend and Mrs. Donald Canty* answered the call and became missionaries to Carver Foreign Missions, Liberia, West Africa. I do not know how many years Naomi Doles served on the field with Carver Missions, maybe 11-15 years, but our paths crossed once again in 1975 in Sinoe County in Liberia, West Africa at a place called Bessmen Town deep in the bush.

Luther Mitchell waited for her while she finished her commitment to Carver Missions. Upon her return from Liberia and her term with Carver Missions being over, they married and returned to Liberia, West Africa under the Church of Christ Holiness Denomination Foreign Mission Board headquarters in Jackson, Mississippi. The first time I saw them they were living in a mud hut in Bessmen Town. Brother Luther Mitchell and his wife were ministering to the

Krone and Sappo tribes in that area and building a house for the missionaries to live in. They may have stayed in Bessmen Town three or four years. I think I visited them once or twice there. The hard work and the heat took their toll on Reverend Mitchell. They moved to Monrovia and the mission bought a house there. Being a builder and a contractor he set out to complete the house and to renovate the part that was already built. Reverend and Sister Mitchell lived in the house as they worked on it and they were there at least 18 months or nearly two years. Catherine E. Jeter and I visited a least once, maybe twice. On our second visit, a year to 15 months apart, Reverend Luther Mitchell did not feel well. We went to the hangout for missionaries in Monrovia, a restaurant called Diana's. The missionaries' fellowshipped every Thursday and enjoyed the food at Diana's. We would take Naomi home after dinner and would have prayer. They left Liberia in March 1981, or so.

Within two months Reverend Mitchell was with the Lord. *Naomi Mitchell* never returned to the foreign field after his death as far as I know, but she became active in America propagating the missionary cause. She remarried and is still alive today and full of fire. Her commitment to the cause of the spread of the gospel of our Lord Jesus Christ has set the standards for the Black faith missionary to follow at the end of the 20th century and well into the 21st century. Naomi Doles Mitchell, "I press toward the mark for the prize of the high calling of God in Christ Jesus," Philippians 3:14.

Missionary #15 Mother Mary Fossett

Mother Mary Fossett is a great missionary at an advanced age. Mother Fossett, a member of the Church of Christ Holiness headquarters in Jackson, Mississippi heard the need of Carver Foreign Missions for a missionary in Monrovia, Liberia. I do not know much about her qualifications, but I do know that she was a music teacher and probably had a degree in music from a school in Mississippi. Mother

Fossett was between the age of 77 and 81 years at the time she sent in her application to the Carver Foreign Missions board. She did not tell them what her age was. When the board saw this multi-talented person's application, they accepted her without seeing her. When she was asked to appear before the mission board she fearlessly came to Atlanta, Georgia ready to go to the field with the Holy Ghost and the gospel. She may have spent five years on the field maybe more, maybe less. What I remember was her zeal and her determination. It taught me that older saints could get the job done. Her years on the field may have been 1969-1973; they may have been 1980-1986 or 1987.

I cannot remember the time, but what I do remember about Mother Mary Fossett was her fearlessness to evangelize in hard places. Almost every Sunday at 4:00 pm, she went to a place called West Point at the waterside and market grounds in Monrovia, Liberia. Mother Fossett along with *Cora McCleary* and *Mable McCombs* preached the gospel in that rough area where many men would not go. I was fascinated to see her chase these men down and tell them of the love of Jesus Christ and see them give their hearts to the Lord Jesus. Mother Mary Fossett was truly an unknown soldier, but known to our Lord Jesus Christ, "I must work the works of him that sent me, while it is day: the night cometh, when no man can work." St. John 9:4.

Mother Mary Fossett's sacrificial life on the foreign mission field should inspire many who knew her. She is with the Lord now, but her deeds in missions will live on. The history of Carver Foreign Missions will tell the full story of what Mother Mary Fossett, Senior Missionary did. She was a great missionary and a senior citizen full of fire and the Holy Ghost.

Missionary #16 Mother Cora B. McCleary

Cora McCleary is one of the pioneer missionaries with Carver Foreign Missions work in Liberia West Africa. She was the teammate of Naomi Doles, and together they founded the Monrovia Bible Institute and College. They also founded the Carver Christian Academy in Painsville at King Gray Village, 9-11 miles outside of Monrovia.

Cora was with Naomi Doles in training at Salala Missions in Gbong County, Liberia deep in the bush. Reverend Edith Johnson was their trainer. *Reverend Malverna Harris* and *Reverend Ella Carol* taught them of the things of mission life and village living. After about a year of training, Sister Doles and Sister McCleary probably with the help of Reverend Montrose Waite and Reverend Edith Johnson started a grade school at King Gray Village in Painsville about 9-11 miles outside of Monrovia and they also founded the Monrovia Bible Institute on Benson Street in Monrovia. The work was very hard.

There was much opposition to their work in the village, as the leaders did not want education (books) in their village. They worked tirelessly many long hours with bad or no equipment. *Reverend Howard Joes,* a member of the Billy Graham team, had a house at the ELWA Mission Station across the road from the tribal grant land that the chief of King Gray Village had given to Carver Missions. The house was located about a half to three-quarters of a mile walk to King Gray Village where these two ladies held school daily, planted a church, conducted Sunday morning and evening services, prayer meetings on Wednesday nights and Sunday School at 9:30; each Sunday they had Sunday School. A mission house was built and some other missionaries joined the work for instance, *Mary Stephen* a Baptist lady from Atlanta, Georgia and *Mable McComb* from Greenville, South Carolina an AME church missionary, *Sister Henrietta Hearn* from Prentiss, Mississippi etc.

Mother McCleary was in everything: church planter, field leader, mission director, Bible school professor and Christian education, etc. Sister McCleary and her team were probably the hardest working missionaries I have ever known. She was active in the Youth for Christ Radio Ministry. Each Saturday night, as a member of the Carolleers, she sang the songs of Jesus Christ on the radio, TV and the Presidential mansion, and had great impact in Liberia. She had an old car, not much support, but she was very effective. She is still alive probable at the time of this writing she is over 75 years old. She may be 81 or 82 at this point, maybe even older. She was asked to retire at her advanced age. Mother McCleary must have had 38-42 years of active missionary ministry. A graduate of Carver Bible College in Atlanta, Georgia and a native of Chattanooga, Tennessee she calls Brooklyn, New York her home. The name of this faithful missionary has been burned into the annals of Black faith mission history as an unblemished record of consistency and much fruit bearing for Jesus Christ our Lord. *Cora McClary* was an outstanding missionary for Carver Foreign Missions in Atlanta, Georgia working in Liberia, West Africa.

Missionary#17 Reverend Dennis Leon Foster

Reverend Dennis Leon Foster, Philadelphia, Pennsylvania is a member of the Nazarene Baptist Church, Philadelphia, Pennsylvania. Reverend Foster was an independent missionary to Japan. His ministry to evangelize the Japanese people spanned 32 years. He began his work with an existing mission board and with missionaries that were there while he was in the United States Army in 1955. In those days, no white mission boards would accept Black American Christians as missionaries. In 1956, Brother Foster began his evangelistic ministry at Abanazawa and Yonogata, Japan. The burden to win the souls of the Japanese to Jesus Christ was overwhelming. Evangelism and church planting was his desire and ministry. He came home a few times on furlough, when he was in the service, I would imagine, that his life was totally committed to his ministry. Reverend Dennis Foster is probably the only Black American Christian missionary man to work as a full-time missionary in Japan.

There may be others that I do not know of that were there. There may have been some Black American Christians as short-term missionaries in Japan mostly college students teaching English as a second language.

Dr. Rhonda F. Jeter, my daughter, was one of those short-term missionaries, through the summer of 1978-1980. She lived in that culture, worshipped at a Japanese church, and taught English there as a student from Taylor University Upland, Indiana.

Mission history must record that the hearts of many Black Christians were open in the 1950s and 1960s, but with no Black mission boards geared to send them there was no open door. Let us look at the qualifications of this great independent Black missionary to Japan:

1. He was saved a the age of 13 at the Nazarene Baptist Church in Philadelphia;

2. He was active in the church from his youth; youth prayer band, youth choir, Sunday school teacher, Baptist training union leader, and he played the organ and the cello;

3. He served in the U.S. Army

4. He graduated from high school and Christian college

5. His life verse Psalms 126:6 "He that goeth forth and weepeth, bearing precious seed, shall doubtless come again with rejoicing, bringing his sheaves with him.;"

6. His life may have been touched by the ministry of Reverend Montrose Waite, missionary to Liberia who was also a member of the Nazarene Baptist Church of Philadelphia.

Reverend Foster was also supported by the Nazarene Baptist Church Foreign Board or Society, the *Carrie J. Lee* and *George Roy* Missionary Society of the Corinthian Baptist

Church in Philadelphia, Pennsylvania, his family and friends. Undaunted by the racism in the White evangelical mission organizations in the 1940s through the early 1970s, Dennis Foster by faith was faithful to his call to the Lord Jesus Christ his Master and Lord. He was faithful to present the gospel to the lost in Japan. On April 6, 1989 he was called home to heaven. "I have fought a good fight, I have finished my course, I have kept the faith." II Timothy 4:7. Exerts from his memorial service, obituary, and the help of *Catherine E. Jeter, Carrie J. Lee* and *Georgia Roy* Missionary Society, Corinthian Baptist Church of Germantown in Philadelphia area was a blessing.

Missionary#18 Doctor Henrietta Herron

Henrietta Herron is from a Baptist church in Prentiss, Mississippi. She is a graduate of Carver Bible College in Atlanta, Georgia, and Sister Herron is probably the third full-time missionary to minister with Carver Foreign Missions. Our sister has been involved with all aspects of mission work for over 40 years. Her work at the Monrovia Bible Institute in the early days was relentless. Sister Herron also worked at the mission school that became Carver Christian Academy for many years. Sister traveled into Monrovia in the late evenings to teach Bible doctrine, Christian education and other related subjects 2-4 nights a week. Her ministry was very effective. The equipment was old (old cars and old mimeograph machines), sometime no light at the school or on the mission, in addition there was always a fight with malaria. The Carver Christian Academy was the work early in the day and the Bible Institute was the work at night. The very, very hard work, the very, very hot weather, plus the general hardship of mission work took its toll on her. Her workload consisted of the following:

1. A Bible teacher in the Bible Institute teaching many subjects;

2. An elementary school at the Carver Christian Academy; King Gray Village nine miles outside of Monrovia;

3. Working with youth for Christ Radio Broadcast each Saturday night;

4. Mentoring many students and she loved the Liberian people;

5. Working in the church and the Sunday school at the church planted in King Gray Village;

6. Singing with the Carollers on a national radio broadcast weekly;

7. Soccer coach at the Carver Christian Academy etc.

You name it, she did it.

Sister Herron left the field after many years of service because of illness, but her heart remains in Liberia, West Africa. She has made several trips back to Liberia, and at this point, Henrietta Herron is doing mission work with Rural Services in rural Mississippi in the United States. Without called and committed and people like Sister Henrietta Herron, the work of the spread of the gospel of Lord Jesus Christ would suffer.

Stand-up, Stand-up for Jesus, Romans 1:15-16, "So, as much as in me is, I am ready to preach the gospel to you that are at Rome also. For I am not ashamed of the gospel of Christ: for it is the power of God unto salvation to every one that believeth; to the Jew first, and also to the Greek."

In 2002, Henrietta Herron was given an Honorary Doctor of Divinity Degree from Carver Bible College in Atlanta, GA. As Romans 1:15-16 states, "As much as in me is, I am ready to preach the gospel." She is still alive, still on fire for the Lord doing mission work in a rural area outside of Jackson, Mississippi. She is a great lady, Dr. Henrietta Herron.

Missionary #19 Reverend Willie and Mrs. Betty Qumby

Reverend and Mrs. Willie Qumby were missionaries with the Afro-American Missionary Crusade, Philadelphia, Pennsylvania, the first Black faith mission board established in America. I am not sure when Reverend Willie Qumby and his wife Betty went to Liberia West Africa, but I do know that they did. They worked on the Bopolu Bible Mission Station about 60-65 miles North of West Monrovia in Loffa County deep in the bush. They may have worked between 1960 and 1965 because when I reached Bopolu Bible Mission in January or February of 1966 they were not there. I know that they were from the New York City area and they probably are fruit from the ministry of *Reverend Montrose Waite* or *Dr. Ernest L. Wilson*.

The Qumbys had a diversified ministry at Bopolu Bible Mission: pastoring the church, teaching grade school daily and training preachers in village evangelism. There was also work to do in or at the orphanage on the mission station. Let it here be stated that the primitive conditions that were there at the mission must have been a great obstacle to the Qumby's, and the cultural shock must have overwhelmed them. They had well or creek water to boil and drink. The road was so bad that someone only went down to Monrovia for mail once a month in the dry season; in the rainy season someone went down for mail once every two months. The food was canned meat, fish or vegetables, or they ate African food; fresh local fish, some dry fish called bony, potato greens, collard greens, okra, cassava greens cooked in palm oil plus there was plenty of rice. There was no refrigerator on the station in the early days; candles, kerosene lamps and wood fires were for cooking.

Despite the hardships and cultural shock the Qumbys did a good job in a hard place. Souls were saved and the gospel was preached. Mother Dorothy Evans and Mother Martha Thompson of Philadelphia, Pennsylvania may have ministered with Reverend Willie and *Sister Betty Qumby*. It is said that they returned to America after one term. Their ministry of sacrifice and blessings are placed in the annals of Black mission history. "For the which cause I also suffer these things: nevertheless I am not ashamed: for I know whom I have believed, and am persuaded hat he is able to keep that which I have committed unto him against that day," II Timothy 1:12.

Missionary #20 Reverend Ruffis Prunty

Reverend Ruffis Prunty, Bethany Baptist Church, Pittsburg, Pennsylvania, missionary to the National Baptist USA, Bassa National Baptist Church of Liberia Dr. and Mrs. Horton of Monrovia, Liberia. Reverend Ruffis Prunty was sent to Liberia in the early 1950s. He may have come earlier maybe right after World War II. His ministry lasted for many years. He must have worked with the National Baptist Convention USA early in his ministry in church planting, Christian education. If I'm not mistaken he ministered through agriculture and evangelism at Suhen Mission 20 miles outside of Monrovia and maybe at Bendue Mission at Cape Mount Liberia. He also must have worked at the National Baptist Convention USA Mission Station outside of #1 Gate Grand Bassa County, because he was later active with Reverend Horton who founded a Baptist work among the Bassa tribal people in Monrovia, and in Grand Bassa County planting churches, doing evangelism, teaching grade and agricultural school.

I met Reverend Prunty in the 1980s at an advanced age. He was still doing what God had called him to do many years ago preaching the gospel on foreign fields. My wife Catherine E. Jeter and I had lunch with him and his wife maybe in 1987 or 1989 in Monrovia. I heard around 1994 that he went to be with the Lord. "Also I heard the voice of the Lord, saying, Whom shall I send, and who will go for us? Then said I, Here am I; send me." Isaiah 6:8. Ruffis Prunty was an unkown Black missionary, from Bethany Baptist Church, Pittsburgh, Pennsylvania, National Baptist Convention USA, and Baptist Bassa Ministry under Reverend Horton in Liberia, West Africa.

Missionary #21 Reverend Eugene Thornly

Reverend Eugene Thornly, Philadelphia, Pennsylvania was a missionary in Sierra Leone and Guinea, West Africa under the Christian and Missionary Alliance Mission. He was one of the few Black American missionaries with that mission. He was a contemporary of *Reverend Montrose Waite* and *Anita Bolden Fitts*, so that means he was out somewhere between 1922 and 1939. He must have worked with them between 1922 and 1935. Where he was from I do not know. I do know that he settled in Philadelphia and was a member of Afro-American Missionary Crusade Mission Board, the first Black faith mission. He was a preacher, Bible teacher and a humble man of God. How long he served, I do not know, but as far a I can tell, he did not return to the field after his first or second term.

Reverend Eugene Thornly died in Philadelphia in the late 1960s or early 1970s. I met him at Reverend Waite's mission house in Philadelphia, Pennsylvania. I also think he was a pastor in an AME church outside of Philadelphia in a place called Elmwood, Pennsylvania. Reverend Eugene Thornly truly is a unknown soldier. So send I you to serve unpaid, unknown.

Missionary #22 Elizabeth Proctor

Elizabeth Proctor is from Portland, Oregon. She was a member of the Maranatha Church of God under *Wendall Wallace*. Elizabeth Proctor is a great missionary. She is fruit from the ministry of *Sister Grazelle Settles*. She was a member of the Maranatha Christian Center in Portland,

Oregon. In 1960 when Grazell Settles and Augusta Tyler went to Liberia West Africa, Sister Proctor was left behind.

In 1967, I met her for the first time at a Saturday night church meeting in Portland, Oregon. My family and I were out trying to raise funds to get Grazelle Settles a Land Rover (a four wheel drive jeep) for her work, 200 miles in the deep bush in Liberia, with no transportation. My wife and our five children were with me on that fund raising trip. The funds were to be sent to a sister in Philadelphia, *Letha Festus*, and then sent on to Sister Settle for the purchase of the vehicle. At this meeting, I showed slides and spoke about the needs of Sister Settles and the Voice of Africa Mission.

In 1969 in September or October, I made by myself another trip to Portland, Oregon to show the supporters the picture of the Land Rover that Sister Settles had purchased. This time they asked me to preach at the church on Friday night. There was a big crowd of people there. Being filled with the fire from my recent ministry in Liberia and the Ivory Coast, I gave an alter call for missionaries to labor for the Lord Jesus Christ anywhere in the world. A large group came forward and in this group was Elizabeth Proctor. I took her name and talked with many people and left the area with joy. Sister Proctor was a young nurse and loved the Lord.

In May of 1970, I returned to Liberia, West Africa and traveled 200 miles to the Voice of Africa Mission deep in Grand Bassa County. When the truck I was riding in stopped at the Voice of Africa Mission property, the first person I saw was Elizabeth Proctor she said, "Brother Jeter don't you remember me? I came forward in that meeting last September." I said, "What are you doing here?" She said, "The Lord led me here to help minister with Mother Tyler and Mother Settles."

The work that Elizabeth Proctor did at the Voice of Africa Mission is as follows: teacher and principal at the mission school, Bible teacher, nurse to the area and mission, served as house mother to the girls at the boarding school on the mission, teaching adult education, preaching on the mission and in the village outreach etc. Sometimes she was mission director when Mother Tyler and Sister Settles were on furlough.

In 1973 or 1974 Elizabeth Proctor left Liberia, West Africa and after a brief rest in America she became a missionary in (Haiti) West Indies deep in the mountains there. As far as I can tell, Elizabeth Proctor has spent at least 30 continuous years as a faith missionary ministering the word of God, winning souls and meeting the needs of people. She's still in (Haiti) at the time of this writing, March 29, 1999. "The people answered him, we have heard out of the law that Christ abideth for ever: and how sayest thou, the Son of man must be lifted up? Who is this Son of man? St. John 12:34.

Missionary #23 Reverend Claude and Althea Austin

Reverend Claude and Mrs. Althea Austin, they were from a Baptist church in Mansfield, Ohio, but worked with the Kodish Church of Emmanuel out of Pittsburgh, PA. Their mission work was at Killingsworth Mission in Todee, Liberia. The story of Reverend Claude and Althea Austin is one that is very difficult to tell, because of the many disappointments they faced before they arrived on the field in Liberia, West Africa in the Todee area. Reverend Claude Austin must have stayed on the field 6 ½ -7 ½ years, his wife Althea Austin maybe 9-11 years or longer maybe 12.

Reverend Austin was a farmer, preacher and administrator etc. Also, he was a builder and a Bible teacher. Althea Austin was a great missionary in the Christian and Missionary Alliance Church. She was a teacher, preacher, school administrator, field director etc. I met Reverend and Mrs. Austin for the first time in Bridgeville, Delaware in the late September or early October 1967 at a workers' prayer conference that was held at the only Colored Christian and Missionary Alliance Church in the State of Delaware. The pastor's last name was Shields. He was a brother who had tried to plant a Christian and Missionary Alliance Church among Blacks in Philadelphia area, but moved to Bridgeville, Delaware to establish a church there..

As traditions went, the Colored or Black Christian and Missionary Alliance Churches would have a prayer conference at one of their churches for a week each year. There were Colored Christian and Missionary Alliance Churches in Pittsburgh, Cleveland, Overland Ohio, Strousburg, Pennsylvania and a few other places in the United States. Most of the Black missionaries in America would try to attend these prayer conferences every year. These prayer conferences were very important. Black American missionaries who were home on furlough came to these conferences every year and they usually had a missionary speaker along with a preacher in the prayer conference.

Every year the missionaries who went home on furlough would attend if they had belonged to a mission ministry or had retired. There was a strong union between the Black Christian and Missionary Alliance people, the Afro-American Missionary Crusade and other Blacks in world missions, because not too many Blacks went to the foreign mission field. In 1967, *Dr. Joseph C. Jeter Sr.* was the mission speaker for the conference Wednesday through Sunday afternoon. On Thursday or Friday night, Reverend and Mrs. Austin and their two grandchildren Petee and Mark arrived. They were joyful because they were candidates to go out to Malawi in East Africa to minister as missionaries as a family. I finally began to ask them questions about shots, visas, passports etc. They had not heard of these things before. I told them that I would help them to get ready to go, but I did not think that the board, which had promised to send them, would send them out.

In the course of the next few years, I made many trips to Mansfield, Ohio to get them ready. Finally, they had most of what they needed to go, but no appointment from the mission board that they had applied to. One Wednesday night, I got a phone call from Reverend Austin asking for direction. The Kodish Church of Emmanuel had called and asked them to go out to Liberia, West Africa to work on their mission station in Todee, Liberia about 54 miles in the bush from Monrovia Liberia, immediately. We talked that night about opened doors and closed doors etc. I told Reverend Austin to go through the open door. I also said to him he would never be accepted at his age as a first term missionary from the mission he had applied to. Reverend Austin was between 59 and 65 years old at that time. He wanted to go to East Africa; this door was opened to West Africa. Reverend and Sister Austin traveled overnight from Mansfield, Ohio to Philadelphia to ask the board that they had been accepted under if and when they were going to go to Malawi. They were told that day that they would not be going to Malawi; they were too old. The door was closed. They hurried back to Mansfield, Ohio and ran through the opened door. The commissioning service was set. A plane ticket was purchased for Sister Austin, as a missionary she was needed quickly at the Kodish Mission in Todee. She went by air and Reverend Austin and his two grandsons followed by ship. It was a great joy to travel from Philadelphia to New York City to pick them up and take Reverend Austin and his two grandchildren, to Brooklyn New York Harbor and watched them sail away to the mission field. That must have been in July 1969 or 1970. Praise the Lord!

When I arrived in Liberia in the Spring of 1971, I found my happy friends working on the field. The church was in good shape, the school was doing well, and crops had been planted (rice, pepper, cassava, collard greens, garlic etc.). Claude had been going to the villages deep in the bush, walking six hours to preach. People were getting saved. Reverend Austin was a great blessing as a Black man on the mission field. He may have been out 5-7 years. He got sick, and came back to Pittsburgh then went to be with the Lord.

After the death of Reverend Austin, Mother Althea Austin returned to the mission field at Todee and continued her ministry at an advanced age. Her ministry may be from 1970 or 1971 through 1985. Mother Austin is still alive at the time of this writing March 11, 2003. She is the oldest Black American missionary living today. A small denomination with a mission burden, the Kodish Church of Emmanuel is outstanding. As far as I know, the mission station at Todee is open today. Reverend Claude and Althea Austin were great, great missionaries. "Pray ye therefore of the Lord of the harvest, that he will send forth laborers into his harvest," Matthew 9:38.

Missionary #24 Reverend Douglas and Dorothy Oliver

Reverend and Mrs. Oliver were the first Black American missionaries to work on or in the subcontinent of India that I know of. I think they worked there from 1957-1966, it may have been more, or it may have been less. They worked among the Hindus, Muslims, and tribal people etc. doing church planting and other related ministries. Reverend and Mrs. Oliver and their children are a testimony as independent faith missionaries.

I know that Sister Dorothy Oliver is alive today and she lives in Philadelphia, Pennsylvania. Whosoever, desires might want to do more research on them. They are a mission family who took on a tremendous challenge. Where Reverend Oliver is today I do not know. Mrs. Oliver is a member of the New Covenant Church of Philadelphia at the time of this writing; Bishop C. Milton Grannum is the pastor.

Missionary #25 Mother Pearl Grant

Mother Pearl Grant and husband, Philadelphia, Pennsylvania, Church of the Living God Work in Todee, Liberia 1956-1963. Mother Pearl Grant is from Philadelphia,

Pennsylvania. If I'm not mistaken, she was a member of the New Bethlehem Baptist Church on Aspen and Preston Streets. Mother Pearl Grant went out as a missionary for the Church of the Living God, Bishop White's denomination at 58th and Thompson Streets in Philadelphia.

She did a great work under very hard circumstances in the Todee area of Liberia, West Africa. She may have had her husband working with her I do not know, but I know she planted a church, a mission school and was a viable witness for the Lord Jesus Christ in that area. All of the buildings on the stations were mud and sticks when she started. She started to build a church building made out of concrete block, but was unable to complete it due to lack of money and there are other issues I could talk about. There was much suffering and much sickness there, but she did a work.

When I arrived at the mission in March or April 1966, a young missionary named Iris Johnson was there, and the testimony of Pearl Grant's unfinished church building told a story of hardship, heartache and the suffering of Mother Pearl Grant. She did her best with what she had. I do not think she died there, but her labor of love will remain. It will be 10-15 years before Missionary Mother Carrie Ford would complete the church building. Praise the Lord! "Where there is no vision, the people perish: but he that keepeth the law, happy is he," Proverbs 29:18. Pearl Grant an unknown soldier.

Missionary#26 Mother Martha Thompson
(Afro-American Missionary Crusade)

Martha Thompson is a great missionary. She is still alive today at the time of this writing, March 4, 2003. Martha Thompson is a member of the Mt. Caramel Baptist Church a 57th and Race Street in Philadelphia, Pennsylvania. Sister Martha Thompson is one of the great pioneer missionaries of the Black Faith Mission Era. Her service to the Lord Jesus Christ must span 55 years or more.

Mother Thompson is from the Mt. Caramel Baptist Church, the home church of Mother Gladys East one of the great National Baptist Convention USA missionaries of the 20th century. Martha must have been a member of Christ for Youth, the ministry that *Reverend Ernest L. Wilson* started in the mid-1940s. She must have been touched by the life of *Reverend Montrose Waite*, the founder of the first Black faith mission board in America, because she became one of the young people from the Philadelphia area to become a missionary of the Afro-American Missionary Crusade. The impact of Reverend Wilson and Reverend Waite plus Missionary Gladys East must have moved her.

Where she got her formal academic training from I do not know. I think Virginia Union, but I also think she is a graduate of Philadelphia College of Bible, but I am not exactly sure. Her Bible training may have come from Philadelphia College of Bible. Martha was able to teach Bible and grade school.

The time that she went to the field must have been in the mid-1950s, because I found her on Bopolu Bible Mission when I arrived in March or April 1966. Sister Thompson is a kind, tender and loving person. She is a bush preacher, principal of the school at Bopolu Mission and Sunday school teacher etc. She also gave much help to the orphanage ministry. At the time of this writing, April 9, 1999, she was still alive; maybe she lives in Richmond, Virginia. Her burden for souls, her walk of faith and her earnest commitment to Jesus Christ could be seen in her.

Mother Thompson did much to show people on her field the love of Christ. When she left the field, I am not certain. It was probably in the mid-1980s. Martha was active at Bopolu Bible Church, you name it, she did it. She helped develop the African preachers at the church. Sister Thompson worked tirelessly at the mission office in Philadelphia after many years on the field. She was quiet, prayerful and effective in her ministry. Praise the Lord! The people in the area of the Bopolu Town have seen in Missionary Martha Thompson a witness for Jesus Christ. "For to me to live is Christ, and to die to gain," Philippians 1:21.

Missionary #27 Reverend Andrew D. Trustee and Irma Marie Trustee

The Trustees' are from the Greater Philadelphia area. They served with their young family with the Afro American Missionary Crusade, the First Black Faith Mission Board in America. Their ministry at Bopolu Bible Mission was outstanding. Reverend and Mrs. Andrew Trustee did many things at the mission.

Sister Marie Trustee, a registered nurse along with Dorothy Evans worked at the mission clinic. There were no doctors in the Bopolu area, so Sister Trustee ministered to the sick in that area. Also, Sister Trustee may have taught at the elementary school on Mission.

Reverend Trustee was everything at the mission; Bible teacher, mission builder, pastor of the Bopolu Bible Church, village preacher etc. He walked to different towns each afternoon to preach the Word of God. Some of the mission towns that he preached at are as follows: Vonguma, Soploma, Toloqulie and many others. For many years he was the only man on the mission.

By trade, Brother Trustee was an electrical engineer and gave his all to the ministry. Reverend Trustee gave eight years on the field at Bopolu. He is one of the group of Black missionary men that took his family to the deep bush to minister the Word of God.

When he returned home in 1974, he did not ever return to the field again, but stayed at home championing the needs for the mission. He is one of the valued men of Manna Bible Institute, Philadelphia, PA. Many good things stand out in my mind about Reverend Andrew Trustee. I will share a few of them: First, he was willing to suffer for the gospel sake. I remember Reverend Trustee at the creek on the Bopolu Bible Mission getting rocks to reinforce one of the mud and stick buildings at the mission. He had an old wheel barrel and a broken shovel or maybe no shovel. At any rate, the rocks were put in the wheel barrel and he carried them up to the old building to mix with cement and fixed the foundation of the building. He achieved this without basic equipment. Reverend Trustee had a great ministry and ministered faithfully to his family at meals and in daily devotion. Reverend and Sister Trustee took one of Have Christ Will Travel Ministries short-term missionaries from America to work with them at the Bopolu Bible Mission around 1971 or 1972. Second, Reverend Trustee was a man of principle. He walked with the Lord. He helped other missionaries and he preached and taught with power. Andrew Trustee went to heaven Saturday, May 1, 1999. II Timothy 4:7. "I have fought a good fight. I have finished my course. I have kept the faith." He was one of the great Black missionary men of our time. Reverend Andrew Trustee.

Missionary #28 Reverend Barbara Harper

Reverend Barbara Harper, Kodish Church of Emmanuel, Pittsburgh, PA.

Reverend Harper worked for the Kodish Church of Emmanuel Missions Station in the Todee area of Liberia, which is 26 miles from the Firestone Rubber Plantation Gate #4 about 70 miles from Monrovia, Liberia in the deep bush.

I do not know how long Reverend Harper served in Liberia. She was there when I arrived in March or April of 1966. She had other missionaries with her, and they were all living in an old mud and stick house with no toilet or running water etc. This mission was deep in the bush. Why was Reverend Barbara Harper there? To minister to the Gospel of Jesus Christ in that area. Sister Harper was on a team of integrated missionaries. There was Sister Frances Watkins and her two children and a white missionary by the name of Bonnie Cleaver. I will speak more about this at a later time.

Sister Harper had a large ministry; preacher, teacher, mission administrator, school principal and other works. She taught in the bush and planted churches in villages. She did work for the Lord. How many terms she served I can not tell, but she was very effective in her work. Upon her return to America in the late 1960's or the early 1970's she obtained another college degree in Administration or Nursing. Her ministry was that of a mission advocate and recruiter for the Kodish Church of Emmanuel while in the United States. She died in the late 70's or early 80's.

She was a young woman who made a great contribution to the effort of the Black church in foreign missions. Phillipians 4:13. "I can do all things through Christ which strengthens me." The life in the mud and stick house ended in late 1966 when three white brothers from mid-Pennsylvania completed the mission house. I can remember two of the three men's name; Roy Asper and Bobbie. I don't know Bobbie's last name. And there was another man, but I can not remember his name either. This was truly a labor of love provided by these men.

Missionary #29 Mother Francis Watkins
(Killingsworth Mission, Liberia)

Francis Watkins, Pittsburgh, PA.

Francis Watkins and her two children, I can not remember their names; a boy and a girl. They were in the mix of ministering, and were a family team of missionaries. They went to school and church as a family on the mission. Sister Watkins had a great ministry as a Bible teacher, preacher and a great prayer warrior and administrator.

Along with the magnificent holy life, Sister Francis worked hard. Her ministry in Liberia with the Kodish Church was from nine to 15 years, maybe more. Her work was great!

Along with all the work that she did, the mission had a clinic that was opened once or twice a week. Sister Watkins along with Barbara Harper and Bonnie Cleaver worked as a team in the clinic. The story of the ministry of Francis Watkins, her children and her two teammates in the deep bush is a spectacular event in mission history.

Francis Watkins is with the Lord. Her children are still alive and the work of the Kodish Church mission is still alive. Thank God for fearless, holy women like Mother Francis Watkins. Mother Francis Watkins was committed missionary from 1964-1985.

Missionary #30 Ruby Clark

Ruby Clark, Dayton Ohio, United World Mission Board

Ruby Clark ministry was in Mali, West Africa and Senegal West Africa. Her work was 28 – 35 years long. Sister Clark did church planting and school work in Mali West Africa, as well as women's ministry in Senegal, West Africa. Her church and women's work in West Africa was outstanding.

Ruby Clark is now retired from the work in West Africa, but now represents the African Church in the United States and raises funds to support the church and pastors in Senegal, North Africa.

The impact of the ministry of Ruby Clark is one of the only Black American Christian missionaries to work in Mali and Senegal for over 30 years. She is also one of the few Black Americans to work in Senegal with Muslim women in the 20th Century. I met Ruby a few times at Mission Conferences in United States. Ruby is one of the few Black missionaries that worked for many years with a white leadership mission in the United States. Ruby is loved and well received by her mission family. Ruby Clark is from Dayton, Ohio. Romans 8:28. "And we know that all things work together for good to them that love God. To them who are all called according to his purpose."

Missionary #31 Reverend Walter and Vera Gibson, UPC Foreign Missionary (UPC, United Pentecostal Council of the Assemblies of God, Cambridge, MA)

The UPC is a Black American Pentecostal Denomination. Their headquarters is in Cambridge, MA. They have mission work in Liberia West Africa and in the West Indies; Barbados and other places therein.

Reverend Walter and Reverend Vera Gibson were missionaries from Hollis, Long Island, New York. Bishop Robert Caesar Sr. in Hollis, New York. The name of their church is Bethel Gospel Tabernacle.

Reverend Walter and Reverend Vera Gibson's ministry in Liberia began in the early 1960's. I met them at Bonnika Mission in Cape Palmas, Liberia. They were ministering to the Grabo Tribe and building a large church, deep in the bush. Their ministry was church planting, evangelism, Christian education, and preaching. How many years they stayed I do not know, but they left the field in the fall or winter of 1967. So they were there three to five years. They did much work. They were a dedicated couple who endured many hardships. They returned to America and were doing church planting in Long Island, New York.

Missionary #32 Mother Pearl Page

Pearl Page, Church of God in Christ Missionary, Tubucka Mission, Liberia West Africa, in the Cape Palmas area, South Liberia.

Mother Pearl Page is from Salinas, California. Her home church is in Seaside California. Pearl Page's ministry in Liberia must have spanned eight to ten years. Her work was church planting, Christian education, evangelism, administration etc. The mission at Tubucka had a church, elementary boarding school and she did much ministry and preaching.

Mother Page started her work in 1958, and it lasted for at least three terms. She must have left Liberia in 1967 or 1968. When I returned to the area in 1969 she was not there.

There was much sacrifice and much suffering in those days for Black missionaries. Mother Page invited me there twice for revival meetings; two weeks each time.

It was at Tubucka Mission that I began to learn of the plight of the Black missionaries in 1966. The work that Mother Pearl Page has done will never be forgotten. Pearl Page, an unknown missionary soldier.

Missionary #33 Dorothy Webster Exhume, Haiti, West Indies, Church of God and Christ

Dorothy Webster Exhume is a marvelous missionary. I do not know when Sister Webster began her ministry in Haiti. I met Sister Exhume in Port au Prince, Haiti in September of 1966. I would imagine she had been there 10-12 years before, because she had three children; two boys (Franz and Amealcar) and one girl (Mar-Lil). The work that she was directing was large. There were many churches under her jurisdiction and at least one orphanage with many schools and preachers. She lived in Pationville, in a house with much activity; preaching, Bible teaching, pre-school and many other things went on daily.

She was also preaching and teaching out in the mountains. Her work in Haiti may cover 25-40 years. Maybe 45 years.

Sister Exhume was excited to hear that a Black male preacher had come to Haiti from America to see the country and to see about missions and missionaries. She helped house J.C. Jeter. Sr. in a hotel for ten days in 1966 and took me to different places to see the different needs of the Haitian people. The magnitude of the impact of the ministry of the missionary of Dorothy Webster Exhume may never be fully comprehended. She suffered much. Her fundraising and mailing list was taken by false brethren and used to start another work in Haiti. Many other stumbling blocks were put in her way.

She now lives somewhere in the United States. She was a great blessing to Haiti. The estimated dates of her ministry in Haiti are 1955-1995.

#34 Mother Ermma Moreland, Church of the Living God, Philadelphia, PA, Bishop White's Domination, 58th & Thompson Streets

Mother Moreland is from Pittsburg, Pennsylvania. I do not know the age of Ermma Moreland. Ermma Moreland was not the first of the Church of the Living God Missionaries in Liberia. My wife and I are very close to her. Ermma Moreland's ministry as a foreign missionary began late in life. She may be one of the people born out of the Black Christian Missionary Alliance Church. More may be said about the time that I first met Mother Moreland at the Kodish Church of Emmanuel, on Centre Ave in Pittsburgh, PA. I may be wrong. Maybe it was at the Black Christian Missionary Alliance Church in the Hill District. She was in her late 60's or early 70's. She is the sister of Althea Alston the great missionary from Pittsburgh, PA and Mansfield, Ohio. Both of them ministered in the Todee area of Liberia, West Africa.

Sister Moreland got the burden to go to the mission field but may have thought that she was too old to go. But the CLG mission needed a missionary to preach, teach and do administration, deep in the bush in the area of Todee Liberia.

Sister Moreland was six to ten miles from where her sister and brother-in-law were stationed. She answered the call to the ministry at Church of the Living God mission. She was there five to seven years, or more.

Sister Moreland may have been a graduate of the Hardy Bible Institute, Pittsburgh, PA. Mother Moreland preached in the church in the town in the Todee area. She also may have worked at the Kodish Mission. She was the principal, pastor and administrator at the mission school.

My wife Catherine and I were with her as she celebrated her 80th birthday deep in the bush.

One night the local witch doctor was in his traditional country devil costume. Tradition said that no one could look at the country devil and live if he passed by at night. When he comes by all of the people are suppose to hide. One night at midnight, he appeared making much noise to let everyone know that he was coming. He woke up Mother Moreland. She went outside of the mission house and drove the country devil away. When a tribal court brought charges against her because she had broken a tribal law, she told the tribal court she was under the law of God. If the country devil came to her mission again at midnight, she would drive him away again. This was her declaration to the tribal court. After she said, "I'm under the authority of Jesus," and preached the gospel to them, she walked out and continued her ministry. Ermma Moreland, Todee Liberia from 1977-1987.

Missionary #35 Mother Carrie Ford (Church of the Living God Mission)

Mother Carrie Jane Ford was a great missionary and a great Christian. Mother Ford was a hard worker, great educator and a great church worker. Somewhere between 1969 and 1971, Mother Carrie was a short term missionary for CLG Missions in the Todee area in the bush; about 48-57 miles from the Monrovia, Liberia. She saw the need and picked up the burden for the mission and came back home, resigned from her job in York, Pennsylvania school system and was appointed a full-time missionary to the CLG Church mission and returned to Todee, Liberia. She remained there for approximately 16 years, until June 1989.

She was a preacher, Bible teacher, principal of grade school; pre-primer through the six or seventh grade. Mother Carrie Ford could do more with a tambourine than any other person I know. Mother Ford pulled off some of the greatest mission feats, I have ever seen. For instance, she finished the church building that Mother Pearl Grant of Philadelphia started in late 1950's. When I arrived to visit the CLG Mission, in March of 1966, there was an unfinished, large concrete block church. All the rest of the building were mud and sticks. Mother Ford and her co-workers Geraldine Baxter of Stanford, Connecticut, USA were in the Bush for 1-3 years along with Ermma Moreland, Pittsburgh, PA.

Mother Ford also built better schools (classrooms) out of concrete block. She evangelized in the Todee area where the witch doctor and the country devil, as well as witchcraft were prevalent. Mother Carrie Ford loved to have Rev. Joseph C. Jeter and his wife Catherine come to visit, preach and fellowship at the CLG Mission. Mother Ford left the field in 1989 when she was 79 years old. She lived another 12 years. In these 12 years she preached the gospel and preached missions. She loved Christ. Phil 1:21. For me to live is Christ and to die is gain. Mother Carrie Ford.

Missionary #36 Dr. Andrew Foster – World Missionary to the Deaf

Dr. Andrew Foster was a great man of God. I met him maybe 25 years ago at the Bible Institute of Los Angeles (BIOLA) University Missions Conference in La Mirada, California. Dr. Andrew Foster was a missionary to the deaf. He was a blessing to the world. His ministry touched many lives. He was born in 1925 in Fairfield Alabama. The date of his death I do not know, but I do know that he died in an airplane crash in Africa going from one country to another with his ministry to the deaf, teaching and preaching the Gospel. In 1956, he started deaf training in Alabama. He found only 50 special teachers for the deaf to cover the span of 70 million people throughout the world. In most Africa countries, there were not many qualified people to teach deaf people the gospel.

Dr. Andrew Foster founded schools in 19 African countries. His wife Virtue introduced schools of sign language with the idea of physical help and spiritual help for deaf people. Most of the information on Dr. Andrew Foster and I got from Urban Ministry's pamphlets: Heritage personality missionaries today. Dr. Foster was held in high esteem and we did have fellowship with him at BIOLA University Missions Conference many years ago. Not many people know about him. He was a superb missionary with a vision for the handicapped/deaf all over the world. There was a need for them to hear the gospel of our Lord Jesus Christ. St. John 20:21 "As the Father hath sent me even so I send you."

Missionary #37 Sister Josephine Mentor

Sister Josephine Mentor, National Baptist Convention USA. She worked on two fields as a missionary Suhen Mission, Liberia, West Africa in 1960s and at the National Baptist Convention Mission at Churad Zulu Malawi, East Africa outside of the City of Blantyre, Malawi in the late 1960s. I saw her out there in 1970 and 1971, so she probably was in Malawi from 1969 through 1974. The main mission station was at Churad Zulu in Malawi right outside of the City of Blantyre Malawi. The director was Dr. Daniel S. Malekebu. Some of the times and dates may be hazy in my mind, but I know she had nursing experience and she was an administrator, possibly a teacher.

She was at Suhen Mission in the late 1960s. She was a great missionary. She suffered many things and did a great job! Sister Mentor was from the Tulsa, Oklahoma area. I visited her in July 1970 and July 1971. I found her diligent and faithful to her ministry and was the projection of what Emma B. Delaney stood for in Malawi in 1900 through 1905. Whether Josephine Mentor is alive at the time of this writing May 1, 1999, I do not know. This I do know, she served on a hard field and she served well.

Missionary #38 Sister Verna Boman (Kodish Church of Emmanuel, Pittsburgh, PA)

I do not know much about Sister Verna. I do know that she was from Oberland, Ohio. She was probably from the Black Christian and Missionary Alliance church in Oberland, Ohio. She was a nurse, Bible teacher, preacher, and school principal. Her ministry was great and there were many hardships, but she did a great job. She kept the mission with church, clinic and grade school. I do not know the dates of her ministry, but it must have been in the middle of the 1970s. She spent two or three years at the Killingsworth Mission.

I can not remember if I saw her there. I think I did, once or twice on my yearly visit to missionaries in West Africa. What I do know about her is that she did an excellent job as she minister the Word of God in that very desolate place, Killingsworth Mission Todee Liberia. "Lift up the eyes, look on the fields, they are white already to harvest," St. John 4:35. Verna Boldman, a magnificent Black missionary from Oberland, Ohio.

Missionary #39 Mother Naomi Lundee (Church of God and Christ, Monolu Mission, Liberia)

Mother Naomi Lundee is from the Greater Philadelphia area somewhere in South Jersey. Her ministry was at the Church of God in Christ Mission at Monolu, Liberia, about 8-12 miles above Tobucka Mission in Cape Palmus, Liberia in

Maryland County. How long her ministry lasted in Liberia is unknown, but she was very effective. Her work was extensive. Pastor of the church, principal of the day school, director of the mission, and of the outchurch ministry was quite a task. *Bishop Amos Nyma*, Cape Palmus, Liberia was one of her young people. Her ministry in Liberia must have been eight to twelve years; 1956-1965 or 1967.

When I arrived in the area she was in America. Mother Naomi Lundee's work was outstanding. Her work, her teaching was unparallel. With the lack of money, pressing sore upon her, she pressed forward. Her ministry was with the Grabo Tribe and she is still remembered there until this day. Her health broke down, but her eyes stayed on Jesus. She is remembered as an Unknown Soldier that was effective in her ministry.

Missionary #40 Reverend Thomas Clark Carstarphen

Reverend Thomas Clark Carstarphen was a dedicated home missionary. Reverend Carstarphen was a street preacher in Philadelphia and around the United States of America. He was a graduate of the Manna Bible Institute in Philadelphia, PA. He was born in Mobile, Alabama, but moved to Philadelphia.

Reverend Carstarphen served as a missionary under the American Sunday School Union. In 1964 he moved to Fort Valley, Georgia. He started many Sunday Schools on this mission. He planted a church in Warner Robins, Georgia. In 1971 he purchased 88 acres in Jeffersonville, Georgia, the home of Springs of Living Water Camp, Sparttolar Bible Camp. In 1979 he moved to Chattenooga, Tennessee and planted Sparttolar Bible Church and pastured it until 1998 when his health failed.

When returned to Middle, Georgia in the mid '60's, he had a ministry "designed to" develop conferences that would train others in missionary work. Reverend Carstarphen along with a host of other brothers embraced Phillipians 1:21. Dr. Joseph C. Jeter along with Reverend Carstarphen spent much time on the streets of Philadelphia, PA and Georgia performing great works in the name of the Lord.

Reverend Carstarphen was a camp planter, church planter, youth worker, and pastor. He was 76 years of age when he died. Reverend Thomas Clark Carstarphen served the Lord for more than 40 years.

Missionary #41 Doriese Porter (Christian in Action Faith Mission, Freetown, Sierra Leone West Africa)

Doriese Porter was a great young missionary. Her mission started as a teenager in New York City. In her late teens, she was full of fire who led the way for many other young people to commit themselves to Jesus Christ for mission service. Doriese was a member of a Holiness Church and may have been a member of the Church of God and Christ. Her burden caused her to join Christians in Action, then in Long Beach, California. From what I can tell, she minister in London, England and in Freetown Sierra Leone, West Africa. When I arrived in Freetown, Sierra Leone, West Africa in 1969 or 1970 Doriese was not there. She had gone to another field.

Her work included Bible training, personal evangelism, and church planting. Young peoples work. The Africans had not seen many Black American missionaries who were willing to minister to them.

Doriese Porter has since married and returned to the States and is still involved in world mission endeavors. Doriese Porter is a great, great missionary. At the date of this writing, Doriese is still alive and lives in California. Doriese, thank you for your effort to show young people the way of missionary life. She may be the youngest Black full time faith missionary ever.

Missionary #42 Daisie Whaley – W.E.C. International, Fort Washington, PA and Ivory Coast West Africa

W.E.C. International is an independent white leadership faith mission. Daisie Whaley was born in the ghetto of North Philadelphia (near 6th & Race near Vine Streets) and she became a great missionary. She had a Godly mother and a great pastor. (Reverend Ben Johnson, the founder of Christ Baptist Church, Philadelphia, PA where Daisie Whaley was saved.) She had 30 years in the Country of the Ivory Coast in West Africa. For most of the 30 years she was the only Black American Christian Missionary in this country. She is also a graduate of Manna Bible Institute of Philadelphia, PA. Her ministry began in 1968 or 1969 in Ivory Coast. Before she entered the country she went to French speaking Canada for language training in French then on to France for more training, and then in to Ivory Coast where she studied under John and Grace Reeder the Guru language. She became fluent in the Guru language.

W.E.C. International is a total faith mission with white leadership. Each missionary must raise their own support. In July 1969, our first short term missionary (Mr. Joseph Wheeler, Mt. Vernon Baptist Church, Philadelphia, PA) and I went to visit Daisie on the field in Ivory Coast in Africa. She was learning the Guru language. This was the language of the tribe she was going to work with. She was at a mission station in a town called Zuenola in Central Ivory Coast, about 150 miles in the bush. Daisie's ministry included: Bible teaching, preaching in churches, teaching at women's conventions, counseling, Christian camping, teaching girls and young women to walk with God. Daisie

49

was loved by all the people in the area of the Ivory Coast and was respected by those in her mission family. She suffered many things; car stolen and wrecked, many disappointments were forgotten by those at home. While in the field she was visited by Reverend J.C. Jeter and sometimes missionary Catherine E. Jeter in our ministry to missionaries. There are some things that we need to reveal in the ministry of Daisie Whaley : 1) she was and is holy, 2) she is diligent, and 3) she is fruitful. After 30 years in Africa, she is now in America seeking to mobilize Black Christians and Black churches in world missions. She has mobilized two short teams for Nova Scotia, Canada, the summer of 2000 and 2001. Her heart is hot to spread the gospel, St. John 15:16. Her missionary work was exemplary.

Missionary #43 Diane Jeter (Bryant) – Have Christ Will Travel Ministries, Philadelphia, PA

Missionary to Nova Scotia, Atlantic Canada and Bethlehem School of the Bible, Missionary Training Institute, Philadelphia, PA and Bible Club at Yardly, PA.

Her ministry was from 1975-1980. Missionary Diane Jeter in her early teen years had a burden for the souls and ministry much like her mother, *Catherine Jeter*. Diane was a member of a group of young people called Pioneers for Christ and was committed to the urban ministries of the old home mission called the American Sunday School Union. The teacher or missionary assigned to her group was Reverend Earl Moyer of Philadelphia, PA. The group was training to do Sunday schoolwork, youth work, camping, and evangelism etc. Diane earned an advance ETT Certificate at an early age. She went to Carver Bible College and grad-uated in three and half years. At the age of 16, Diane went to Haiti in the West Indies and worked the summer with the Evangelical Baptist Mission of Haiti, Reverend Claude Noel, President. She was the second short term missionary sent out by Have Christ Will Travel Ministries in 1969. In 1970, she led a group of three young people to Haiti, West Indies to work for the summer. Reverend Floyd Wheeler, Mt. Vernon Baptist Church was on that team.

In 1973, just before graduating from Carver Bible College in Atlanta Georgia, Diane was asked by her father if she would give one year to Have Christ Will Travel Ministries to do Bible Club work, children's camp and evangelism among the Black Canadian communities in Western Nova Scotia at Middleton. She said, "Yes" and went out with the summer team in 1975 and stayed in Nova Scotia as a full-time missionary for three years and one year in Philadelphia, PA.

Diane did not have a car and lived in a very small house at the beginning of her ministry. She received almost no support and God began to work miracles. A car was given from a brother from a white Baptist Church near Philadelphia in Huntington Valley, Pennsylvania. The people of Nova Scotia (White and Black) were glad to have a missionary worker amongst them. Her targeted people were the Blacks of Nova Scotia; the field was 240 miles and she ministered to all people.

A team worker was provided (*Lea Vera Jackson*, October through January 1975-1976.) Then another sister came by the name of *Betty Brenson* from the same Bible college. Their three year ministry was one of immense blessing for the people in Nova Scotia; Black and White. Many people were saved. Twenty-eight years later at the time of this writing people are still being blessed as a result of the unselfish work of Diane Jeter.

Diane spent about 17 years teaching at a number of Christian Schools on the east coast of USA. The effort of young missionaries like Diane, Lea and Betty is truly awesome, St. John 3:18. Diane now lives in Rockville, Maryland, has earned a Masters Degree in counseling and is considering going to seminary. Diane is the daughter of *Dr. and Mrs. Joseph C. Jeter*.

Missionary #44 Reverend Elgin and Mrs. Betty Taylor – Christian in Action, Westlake, CA

Reverend and Mrs. Taylor have served the Lord in World Missions for over 40 years. He is the first Black American to head a mix mission agency; Christians in Action. I do know and have interacted with Reverend Taylor at different times at mission conferences in the United States. He is still active. The following information is from his biographical sketch put out by Christians in Action.

Christians in Action, *Reverend Elgin Taylor*, the president and chief executive officer of Christians in Action and is a consultant to churches on evangelism on church development. A native of Hubbard, Texas and the youngest of 12 children. Elgin's initial dream was to sign on with Dodger's baseball team. Instead of signing their contract he signed on with the Marine Corps. While stationed in Okinawa, Japan he received his calling to be a missionary and abandoned his life's dream of playing baseball. After his discharge from the service in 1958, he entered Christian in Action Missionary Training School. Upon graduation he returned to Okinawa where they were together and founded and pastured an English speaking congregation for American service men. He also co-pastured a bi-lingual church for Japanese and American converts. In 1965, the Taylor's left to do pioneer work in Nigeria, but escaped to London, England after the Civil War broke out. In England, they started a church and a one year Bible training program, where over 100 pastors and missionaries were trained over the next 15 years.

Returning to the U.S. in 1980, Reverend Taylor became Executive Vice President of Christians in Action. Two years later, he was elected president and CEO after the retirement of a former president. He became the first Black president of an integrated faith mission in America.

Elgin received his masters of theology degree from International Bible Seminary in Orlando, Florida in 1982. In 1992, he authored the booklet "Black History of Missions" which has become a primary source of information for churches and colleges studying missions. Currently, he supervises 270 missionaries and national workers in 23 fields of service.

Based in Woodlake, California, Christian in Action has a four week training session to prepare believers that have a genuine missionary call on their lives. They have missions established in Latin America, Europe, Africa and the Far East. Missionary service can be from one to eight weeks summer mission projects to full-time careers. Reverend Taylor is now retired and is the president emeritus of Christians in Action. A great missionary life committed to the work of God.

Missionary #45 Reverend Carl South – Helping Hand Rescue Mission, Philadelphia, PA

I do not know much about Brother Carl South, but I know he was one of two Black men who ran rescue missions in America. Brother South was a preacher, and a teacher of the Bible. His burden for street people was unusual in the Black Church community. The mission has overnight sleeping facilities, chapel services and food. He worked on his calling in the Tenderloin area in Philadelphia. From what I could tell, he worked at this ministry for 40 years faithfully. I, Joseph C. Jeter and many others use to go the Helping Hand Missions to preach at the nightly services.

I passed by the mission in late December 2001 and noticed that it was closed. I can imagine that Brother South has gone to be with the Lord. I can remember how we would meet at Mission Conferences and talk about ministry. Brother Carl South is one of the unknown Black missionaries who worked and lived by faith. Romans 1:16 He must have labored from the early 1950s to the middle 1990s. He led many to the Lord Jesus Christ. His work is outstanding. II Timothy 4:7. I do not know what church Brother Carl South was from, but I would imagine that he was from one of the Black Plymouth Brethren Assemblies in the Philadelphia area maybe the Calvery Gospel Chapel near 41st and Girard, but I'm not sure. Carl South did a great work.

Missionary #46 Reverend Herbert Rylander – Detroit Rescue Mission, Detroit, MI

Reverend Herbert Rylander was the director of the Detroit Rescue Mission. Reverend Rylander may have been the founder of this mission also. Reverend Rylander had a burden for world of street people, drug addicts, whores and drunks. His rescue mission fed and housed these people. Plus he ministered to them spiritually as pastor, preacher and Christian counselor.

Herbert, along with his wife working along his side, did many things. He also had a burden for world missions and took at least one trip to Liberia, West Africa to visit the Bopolu Bible mission. His work must have spread over 40 or more years. He is now with the Lord. At the time of this writing, February 2002, I do not know if the Detroit Rescue Mission is still open, but this I do know, Reverend Rylander was a doer of the Word and a hero. He lived by faith, Phillipians 4:13.

Missionary #47 Reverend Ronald and Mrs. Betty Stampley

Reverend Ronald Stampley, Sr. and Mrs. Betty Stampley and their family were missionaries with a world view. I first met him at the Los Angeles Bible Training School. The next time I heard of Brother Ronald he and his family were headed out to Turkey under a Black leadership mission. His stay in Turkey was between one and three years. (Probably in the mid 1980s).

In 1989, he and his wife founded a mission called "In His Service Ministries." It was a world evangelistic effort with work at home at the Rose Bowl in Pasedena, CA, in Mexico etc. He also moved with short term teams in east and West Africa.

While planning more world outreaches on a mission trip in South Africa, he went to heaven. The Black mission community mourns the lost of a young man and his vision. Dr. Ronald Stampley born in Chicago, lived in California, got a world vision, worked on it and went into glory. Matthews 9:27-28. Pray ye the Lord of the Harvest?

Missionary #48 Reverend Tim and Mrs. Cecilia McCoy – United Holy Church of America

The McCoys were a husband and wife team and ministered at the United Holy Church of America in Liberia, West Africa. They worked in the northeastern part of Liberia. Their mission must have been above or near Bommi Hills in Bommi Territory. They stayed on their station and worked diligently. Sister McCoy was blind. I do not know if she got water blindness from being in Liberia. She was cheerful and full of the spirit. I never visited their mission station, and I did not see Sister McCoy until she came back to Liberia in the mid 1980s. I do know they were older missionaries and must have been on the field a long time. Reverend McCoy died while repairing the roof on the mission house or school. Their work was about 30 years or more; from the 1950s - 1980s. They were church planters, pastors, Bible teachers, house parents, bush preachers, agriculturalist and farmers.

One outstanding fact about Mrs. McCoy is that she is the only Black missionary that I know of who graduated from Houlton College in Central New York State. The labor of love that Reverend and Mrs. McCoy did is largely unknown, but the labor of love in missions is known by our Lord. Phillipians 3:10. P.S. Reverend Kenneth Thorpe of Bopolu Bible Mission was their friend and helper.

Missionary #49 Reverend Curtis and Mrs. Maves Holmes – West Indies Missions, Haiti West Indies

I met Reverend Holmes in 1969 or 1970. At the time, he was the only Black Missionary working in Haiti with a white mission board. There may have been others, but I don't think so. Brother Holmes was from Detroit, Michigan and a graduate of Detroit Bible College. He was a church planter and also taught in the Bible by Extension Program that the West Indies Mission created to teach Bible to the mountain churches. He was a preacher and did general mission work. He was married and had a little girl. He was on the field for about eight years.

Reverend and Mrs. Homes took in two or three of our short term missionaries (young people) in the mid 70s and guided them through the entire summer. Reverend Home's got sick and he and his family had to return to America. I heard that he and his family were doing mission work in Denver, Colorado. Acts 4:12. He was hard working with a vision. If I'm not mistaken, he is also teaching Bible in Denver, Colorado.

Missionary #50 Sister Iris Johnson – Church of the Living God, Philadelphia, PA

I do not know much about Sister Iris Johnson. I do know she was young during her time in Liberia. She was energetic and diligent. She lived under horrible circumstances at the CLG Mission Station. She had an old car sometimes it ran and sometimes it did not. I think Sister Johnny (as they called her) had been in the U.S. Army or the US Air Force.

The Mission, at the time I arrived March 1966 or 1967, was primitive with only mud and stick buildings and they were old. The trip from Monrovia to Todee Road Junction by Bush Taxi which was very hard, and you did it in two steps: 1) Monrovia to the Todee Road Junction - 33 miles, then you had to wait a long time before moving on to the next Junction, 2) Todee Junction, which took you to the CLG Mission 11-15 miles on dirt road. Her support level was very low.

Her ministry was diversified. She was a preacher, school principal, boarding school supervisor, mission field director, pastor of the church on the mission, and she preached in the bush. Sister Iris Johnson was there when I arrived in 1966. She did a brilliant job. She returned to America in the early 1970s. I saw her once in America in the Philadelphia area speaking at a church in Germantown. Where she is now and what she is doing now, I have no idea. She did her best and is one of the Great Unknown Soldiers of Black American Missions. II Timothy 5:8. I fought a good fight. I have kept the faith. Rev. Iris Johnson, full-time missionary, Church of the Living God.

Missionary #51 Reverend Kenneth Thorpe and Mrs. Jeane Thorpe – AfroAmerican Missionary Crusade, Philadelphia, PA

Philadelphia, PA, Manna Bible Institute Philadelphia, Afro-American Missionary Crusade. The first Black American Mission Board in America headquartered in Philadelphia, PA.

Reverend and Mrs. Kenneth Thorpe ministered at the Afro-American Missionary Crusade Bopolu Bible Mission. The Thorpes were from the ghetto in West Philadelphia. They graduated from Manna Bible Institute and served on the Bopolu Bible Mission Station in Bopolu Liberia. They worked amongst the Keppelle Tribe. They have three children; one boy and two girls. The Thorpes were one of the few Black American Missionaries who took their families with them to the field. The number of years they served on the field must be between seven and 11 years, early and in the middle 1970s. They had an effective and fruitful ministry.

Reverend Thorpe was Pastor, Bible teacher of Bopolu Bible Church, he was field leader of all missionaries, a teacher and preached in the bush villages. Many came to Christ because of his work. He instituted a training program for the men at Bopolu Bible Church to do the work after the missionaries left. His Mission was great. Sister Jean Thorpe likewise had a great ministry, teaching at the mission school and recording and keeping records of their work, teaching Bible in the villages and home schooling their three children later in their ministry. The Thorpes are now home where Reverend Thorpe is pastoring a Bible Church in Camden, New Jersey. He is also the director of the Afro-American Missionary Crusade in Philadelphia, PA. At the time of this writing, the sacrifice and suffering of Reverend and Mrs. Jean Thorpe is not widely known but, they are described in Psalm 126:6. Reverend Ken and Jean Thorpe were magnificent missionaries.

Missionary #52 Reverend Donald and Mrs. Charlotte Canty – Carver Foreign Missions, Atlanta, GA

The story of Reverend and Mrs. Donald Canty is one of astounding faith. Reverend and Mrs. Canty are products of the Liberty Baptist Church in North Philadelphia, Pa., the late Nathanial Crosten, Pastor. *Sister Charlotte Canty* is fruit from Mother Bethel AME Church at 6th and Lombard Streets, Philadelphia, PA. Both are graduates of Philadelphia College of Bible and a number of universities. Reverend Canty received his call to Foreign Missions in late 1964 or early1965. He had applied to Have Christ Will Travel to go to West Africa after Reverend J. C. Jeter returned from Liberia, West Africa in 1966, and upon hearing of the plea for a male missionary to come and to teach Bible at the Monrovia Bible Institute. This plea came from missionary *Naomi Doles*, through J. C. Jeter. Rev. Canty's heart was burdened, he applied and was accepted. He and his family spent 13 years in the Liberia. His wife and family worked as a team. Sister Canty taught at Carver Christian Academy for many years, worked as the mission secretary, plus her job as teacher, and she worked at the King Gray church etc. Reverend Canty preached everywhere and helped all the lady missionaries in Liberia. He was a blessing to the people. His children were with him in the work. Reverend and Mrs. Canty were called by Grace, sustained by Grace and served by Grace. Reverend Donald and Mrs. Canty were members of Christian Stronghold Baptist Church, *Dr. Willie Richardson*, Pastor, Philadelphia, PA.

They are now serving in Atlanta, Georgia as Missionaries. Reverend Canty is the director of the New Birth Missionary Baptist Church Missions Program under Bishop Eddie Long, Pastor. Reverend Canty is also past general director of Carver Foreign Missions, Atlanta, GA. II Timothy 2:2. He has been called to be a Soldier.

Some fruit from the Cantys early ministry is missionary Julia King. In 1977, Julia King was sent out as a short-term missionary from Have Christ Will Travel Ministries to Carver Missions. She completed her Christian education and came back to be a full-time missionary. This is Julia's 4th term.

The Cantys were members of Christian Stronghold Baptist Church in Philadelphia, PA. Dr. Willie Richardson, Pastor. One of the strongest Black Missions minded churches of the modern mid 20th Century in America. Carver Missions also took young short term missionaries from Have Christ Will Travels in the early 1970s.

There is much more that could be said about the Ministry of Reverend and Mrs. Donald Canty. We might say more about their ministry later on.

Missionary #53 Daphne Henderson – Afro-American Missionary Crusade, Philadelphia, PA

Daphne Henderson is from the State of Kansas. Sister Daphne Henderson is a great missionary. Her ministry must be between 30-35 years. She was a member of the Afro-American Missionary Crusade Mission. Mother Henderson was one of the great lady missionaries of the 20th Century. Her work in Liberia, West Africa at the Bopolu Bible Mission was outstanding. She worked with the orphanage that was on the mission station. She was a teacher at the mission school, she preached in the bush at different town lectures in the general area of Bopolu. At one time or another, she may have been the field leader of the mission. Also, whenever she was home on furlough, she brought a mission message to the Black Churches in America. Like most of the Black missionaries in the 1960s through the later 1980s, Sister Henderson had hardships and suffering and she finished her course. Daphne Henderson was an outstanding missionary, Afro-American Crusade, Bopolu Liberia, West Africa. I do remember Daphne being a member of a Baptist church in Kansas and in Philadelphia.

Missionary #54 Dr. Dessie Lee Webster – Fellowship Bible Institute, San Francisco, CA

Dr. Dessie Lee Webster, Founder of Fellowship Bible Institute, San Francisco, California, a member of 3rd Baptist Church of San Francisco, CA, Reverend Amos Brown.

Mother Webster was an outstanding missionary. She is also the first Black American to lead a whole area of the country

(U.S.A.) for Child Evangelism Fellowship Inc, Warrington, MO. Sister Webster was born in Texas, somewhere near Dallas. She is probably the most effective Black home missionary in America in modern times.

Her ministry spanned 70-73 years in Home Mission work. The accomplishments of Mother Dessie Webster on the world mission scene is notable. Eph 2:8. Dr. Webster must have passed into glory around 1984 or 1985. The fruit from her ministry is great. The Fellowship Bible Institute sent two young men out to Liberia West Africa under our mission HCWTM 28-30 years ago. *Revered John Smith, Jr.*, a member of Providence Baptist Church under *Reverend Calvin Jones Sr.*, and *Reverend John Ricky Cannon* a member of Bayview Bible Church in San Francisco. They were sent out as short term missionaries. *Annie B. Walker* and *Maggie Bowden* represent Have Christ Will Travel Ministries in the San Francisco Bay area at the time of this writing, February 25, 2002.

As one of the National Black Evangelical Association (NBEA) - headquartered Portland, Oregon, Founding Members, we commended Dr. Webster for her faithful years of service. The lives of many who studied with her were truly enriched. Her special endowments as teacher, counselor, advisor and friend reached others for Christ regardless of their national origin. Her unshakable faith and the dept of her spiritual convictions and life were used by God to bring about training for thousands of people and salvation for many.

DESSIE WEBSTER was born on May 20, 1904 in the town of Haynesville, Louisiana. Her parents were sharecroppers. Dessie accepted Christ at the early age of nine, in a converted one-room schoolhouse service. The song that was sung was, "Come to Jesus Just Now." She was a graduate from New Hope High school and entered Doss Academy in Emerson, Arkansas. There, she earned a Third-Grade License to teach. She married Daniel Webster on April 4,

1927. From this union a son, Staten, and daughter, Velma, were born. Later, she entered the Southern Bible Training School in Dallas, continuing through graduate school. She was graduated with Honors in 1938. While Dessie and her family were in Dallas, she was trained and inspired by *Portia Marshall Washington Pittman*, daughter of the renowned educator, Booker T. Washington. Her contributions to the community were: Home Missionary, Child Evangelism classes, Miracle Book Club classes for teenagers and adult Bible classes.

During World War II, Daniel went to San Francisco for employment in defense work. The family soon followed. The Holy Spirit continued to guide Dessie as she became a pioneer with the Gospel in the Bay Area, sometimes teaching three times a day. For over ten years, she covered seven Bay Area cities each week. She crossed racial barriers with her spiritual gift, teaching Chinese, Spanish and Caucasian people, as well as African Americans. The Lord led her back to school where she was graduated from Bay Cities Bible Institute, The International Child Evangelism Fellowship, Inc., and the San Francisco Baptist Seminary, receiving a B.A. degree with a Bible major. The Lord kept leading her back to Ministry. This culminated in the organization of the Fellowship Bible Institute in May, 1953. Under her leadership, the school became affiliated with the Evangelical Teacher Training Association, offering extension courses in homes and churches while maintaining a four-year evangelistic program. At age 83, she earned her doctoral degree.

Throughout her life, she received numerous honors celebrating her accomplishments and the many lives she touched. Those who knew her were truly blessed. National Black Evangelical Association (NBEA) dedicated last year's convention to her as the "Mother of NBEA." A highlight of the convention was her regally being wheeled into the banquet hall like the queen she was. A month later, at age 91, the Lord called her home to be in His glorious presence, where we know He said, "Well done, good and faithful servant!"

This tribute has been taken from the NBEA for Dessie Webster. This information was taken from NBEA tribute paper. Mother Webster's ministry was for 70 years.

Missionary #55 Gladys Virginia East – National Baptist Convention USA Missionary, Mt. Carmel Baptist Church, Philadelphia, PA

I met Mother East on my first missionary journey to Liberia, West Africa in 1966. She had been a missionary for many years. Mother East is a member of the Mount Carmel Baptist Church, Philadelphia, Pennsylvania. She was born September 4, 1910 on the Buchanan Mission in Middledrift, South Africa. She was the oldest of seven children. Four of them were born in South Africa to missionary parents, Reverend James and Lucida East. She began her schooling on the mission in South Africa at four and a half years old. By the age of 8 ½ she was able to help the smaller children on that mission.

The rest of her early schooling was in the public schools of Philadelphia. Graduating from Overbrook High and then on to the University of Pennsylvania. She graduated with high honors in 1933. She went on to Women's Medical College in Philadelphia, PA for more training; medicine and laboratory work. Then she went on to Pennsylvania School of Bible and excelled in all of her studies. She also trained at hospitals in other areas of country. Mother East also helped arrange Bible schools in western Pennsylvania and in the state of Mississippi.

In 1944 she answered the call for full-time missionary work at Suein Industrial Mission in Liberia. She spent 34 years in the foreign field in Liberia. Her work included Bible teacher, bush nurse and house mother at the boarding school.

She also taught child care and health practices in villages near the mission stations where she worked. She helped organize a church planning team for evangelism.

Thousands of lives have been touched by her life. Many souls have been saved and many souls have been served by her work. St. John 9:4.

Gladys East was a superb servant of God and spent about 71 years serving him. Portions of this profile are taken from Reflections of her life. Thank you plenty, Mother East.

Missionary #56 Dr. Melvin Banks – Urban Ministries Inc. Chicago, ILL

Dr. Melvin Banks is a great man of God. He is a pioneer in Black Face Christian Literature in the USA and around the world. He is the founder and president of Urban Ministries, Inc. of Chicago, Ill. Because of Dr. Melvin Banks' vision to minister in the area of African American Urban Society the world no longer sees Christianity as the white man's religion. He also ministered to many people around the world.

My wife and I first met Brother Melvin Banks at a regional Mission's Conference in Chicago, IL held by Reverend Ben Johnson of Chicago, IL. All of the attending missionaries were assigned to speak at a local church at 11:00am on Sunday. The Conference was held Friday, Saturday and Sunday. I was to speak at Brother Banks' church. Urban Ministries, Inc. had a Literature Workshop the day before and had left over literature which was to be sent back to their warehouse. I asked for the literature and it was sent to my headquarters in Philadelphia. We used the literature on our fields of Nova Scotia, Canada and the West Indies. In 1989, my wife, Catherine E. Jeter took some of it to West Africa. My wife used the literature to teach in the Bush of West Africa.

We went to visit missionary *Daisie Whaley* in the county of Ivory Coast deep in the Bush in a town called Mancono. Catherine E. Jeter pulled out her Black face charts and pictures from Urban Ministries and began to teach unto them Jesus Christ and the whole of the gospel. Though the pictures and posters were in English, and the people only spoke Gruru and French, the ladies shouted and clapped at the sight of the Black face illustrations of the Bible characters.

From that time on, Have Christ Will Travel Ministries has sent Black face literature around the world; West Africa, Liberia, Ivory Coast, Haiti, West Indies, Kerala State, South West India, Nova Scotia in Atlanta Canada. In Nova Scotia it is used by whites and Blacks alike; Bible clubs, Bible schools and camps and is well received by all.

Dr. Banks and I met in 1987-1989. Many thanks to Dr. Melvin Banks, pioneer missionary, in Black Face Christian Literature worldwide. It's just magnificent to be in an African or Indian country and to witness the fantastic response from the literature produced by Dr. Melvin Banks and his organization.

Missionary #57 Fanney Randolph (Church of God in Christ, Missionary to Haiti, West Indies)

Church of God in Christ, Inc., Philadelphia, PA. Her Ministry in Haiti West Indies was varied. I do not know much about Sister Randolph. I do know that she was committed to the service of the Lord. She probably helped Missionary Dorothy Webster in the vast work of church planting, orphanage work and children's work in Haiti. She lived and worked out of Pationville, Haiti near the Port Au Prince area. The most outstanding thing I remember about her is that she had two boys that are grown men now, with her. Her labor of love will never be forgotten by the people of Haiti and by the Lord. Fanney Randolph gave herself as a drink offering to the Lord. She served unknown on earth but not in heaven. The time of her ministry in Haiti was 1974-1981 or longer. At the time of this writing, February 11, 2003, I do not know where she is, but thank God for her labor.

Missionary #58 Verlene B. Farmer Goatey

Missioanry Verlene B. Farmer served as a missionary with the National Baptist Convention, USA from 1959-1966. For at least two terms she worked at the Suhen Industrial Mission in Liberia West Africa.

She was a teacher of third grade, house mother for a boarding school, village evangelist, taught typing and worked with the children at the school and church. She returned home in 1966 for health reasons. Sister Farmer did outstanding work along as well as with many other missionaries. The missionaries that she worked with are as follows: Mother *Mattie Lee Davis*, Mother *Virginia Antrum*, *Sister Charlotte Levi*, *Sister Berette Stonewall*, *Reverend and Mrs. Ben Stevens* and various other missionaries that worked in Liberia over the years; *Sara Cyrus*, *Reverend John B. Faulkner*, and *Dr. and Mrs. Allen*.

Missionary #59 Theresa Character – Have Christ Will Travel Ministries, Inc., Nova Scotia, Canada

At the time of this writing, February 12, 2003, she has served 25 ½ years on the field. The bulk of her service was in Western Nova Scotia though she has worked all over Nova Scotia. Her work includes; Bible club, Bible camp, home visitation, evangelism, ladies Bible classes and assisting churches.

Sister Theresa pioneered the work in the South Shore area from Liverpool to Shelburne and then over the peninsula from Shelburne to Yarmouth, Nova Scotia. In her pioneer work the distance of her field was 180 miles, or more. She traveled long distances in ice and snow in the winter months; mid October to the last of April.

When the South Shore field was first opened, she suffered much. She lived in an unheated apartment and slept on the floor in a sleeping bag and traveled from Liverpool, Nova Scotia to Shelburn as often as possible in her old car (about 90 miles round trip), because there was no money for heat or furniture in her apartment. She did this for six months. Finally, funds were raised and the Elizabeth Archer missionary residence was bought. A 14'x60' mobile home for $11,000 and she lived in a mobile home park until the land was bought for the mobile home and then moved to 195 Cornwallace Street, Shelburn, Nova Scotia

Her home church, Atlanta Bible Baptist Church, Reverend John McNeal helped a great deal. Berean Bible Baptist Church Atlanta, GA was of great assistance to her ministry and with the purchase of the mobile home. About 18 months later she was moved back to Western Nova Scotia where she is still ministering until this day, February 12, 2003. Theresa is a graduate of Carver Bible College, Class of 1976 and a great young missionary.

Missionary #60 Reverend Uree and Maryann Pullum – All Nations Fellowship Missions, Oakland, CA

I want to describe a few people who never went to the Mission Field but caught a burden for missionary work deep down in Mississippi in the1950s. They moved to Oakland, California and started a missionary support group. The names of these people are the late Reverend Uree Pullum and his wife Maryann.

They founded the All Nations Fellowship Mission in Oakland, CA. The two people I know from this missions are the founders. They began to ministers in this mission as a work of faith. Founded in 1966 by Thelma Brandl, but organized in 1963 under Reverend Uree Pullum and his wife Maryann.

Reverend Uree Pullum and his wife Maryann were from Woodland, Mississippi. The mission raised funds and sent it to people like Dr. Joseph Jeter, Philadelphia, PA and many missionaries from the West Coast. Mother August Tyler, Oakland CA, Mother Maddie Lee Monroe, Dr. Dessie Webster and many others. Reverend Uree and his wife are both with the Lord now, but they are amongst the unknown soldiers.

Missionary #61 Dr. David Cornelius

Southern Baptist Convention, Director of African American Church Relations, and Co-director of International Volunteer Fellowships of the International Mission Board of Southern Baptist Convention, USA

Dr. Davis Cornelius and his family (wife and two children) served for nine years as a missionary in Nigeria, West Africa. Dr. Cornelius was a clean water expert and was sent to Northern Nigeria to do some work in the villages and towns, near Jaws in Northern Nigeria.

He went out as a short term missionary in the 1980s. With his heart burdened with what he saw, he returned to Northern Nigeria with his expertise and the Gospel of Jesus Christ in the mid 1980s – 1990s.

He now serves with the board of the International Missions Southern Baptist Convention, Richmond, VA, February 17, 2003. He has written a paper on African American Christian in World Mission. Praise the Lord for Dr. David Cornelius a great leader in the world of missions and him pioneering water research in West Africa.

Missionary #62 Sister Jacqueline Huggins - Philadelphia, PA, (Wycliffe Bible Translators Mission Board, Hunting Beach, CA)

Jackie is a full-time missionary with Wycliffe Bible Translators. Sister Huggins is a graduate of Fort Wayne Bible College. For 18 years or more, Jackie worked on the island of the Negroes in the Republic of Philippians of Southeast Asia.

Jackie is translating the New Testament from English into a tribal language on the Island of the Negroes. She has been working at this for 16-19 years. The hardship has been many including isolation, but she is almost finished and will move on with Wycliff Bible Translators Board.

Jackie is in the 48-58 old age group, which means that she has been committed to serve in World Missions for a long time. My wife and I saw her many years ago while she was still at Fort Wayne Bible College. Praised the Lord for a spirit filled unknown Soldier Jackie Huggins; a Wycliff Bible Translator.

Missionary #63 Brother Stephen Craig – (Wycliff Bible Translators Mission Board, Progressive Missionary Baptist Church, Berkley CA, Wycliff Headquarters in Hunting, Beach CA)

Brother Stephen, his wife and family (two children) are doing Bible Translation work with a tribal group in Ivory Coast West Africa. Stephen Craig is from the Progressive Missionary Baptist Church in Berkley, CA. Dr. Earl C. Stuckey, Pastor. Brother Craig's wife is a translator also. She is from Ireland. Brother Craig is highly educated and has a great mind. His ministry is about 9-11years in Bible translation. We praise God for Missionary Brother Stephen

Craig, one of three Black missionaries that have worked in Ivory Coast in the last 40 years.

Missionary #64 Reverend Sellers and Sister Mary Jenkins – Light of the World Chapel, Philadelphia, PA

The Jenkins family are one of the many sent out from Light of the World Chapel, Philadelphia, PA. The late Tom Riddley, Pastor Sellers and Mary Jenkins worked as a team. They were trained at Manna Bible Institute, Philadelphia, PA and left Philadelphia, PA 26-28 years ago with their children (four children) and went back to their hometown of Wilson, NC to work as missionaries.

They planted Light of the World Ministries which includes vacation Bible schools, Bible clubs, street preaching, and home Bible classes, nursing home ministries Manna Bible, Institute, Wilson North Carolina and Light of the World Ministries in the same place. Also, Light of the World Baptist Church.

Because of lack of funding he had to become a partial tent maker to care for his family. Their work is a model of what can be done if you are willing to sacrifice and suffer. Reverend Sellers and Sister Jenkins are great unknown soldiers and home missionaries of the 1970s -2000s.

Missionary #65 Norman and Toni Griffin (Abundant Life Bible Missions Petersburg, VA)

Norman and Toni worked as a team. Toni Griffin is a classmate of mine from Philadelphia Bible College, Class of 1964.

They were sent out from Fellowship Bible Church, Philadelphia, PA. The Griffins have been doing home mission work for over 30 years. Their ministry has touched thousands of people around the world. Bible teaching evangelism, reading ministry, Christian camping, church planting and their outreach ministry extend to Central Ivory Coast, West Africa. They also supported missionaries like the late Montrose Waite and Dr. Joseph and Catherine Jeter. Also, missionary Daisie Whaley.

Norman Griffin is the first true tentmaker I have known. He worked all day in Richmond, VA and half the night as a missionary. I wish there was more that I could say about Norman and Toni Griffin and their ongoing ministry. Job 16:19 My witness is in heaven and my record on high.

There are a lot of missionaries that I did not list, not because they are not known, but because I have run out of time. Such as Jackie Everette, Uganda, Michelle Downs, St. Thomas US Virgin Island. Please praise God for those listed.

Missionary #66 Mother Winnie Mae Lane – (Christ Baptist Church, Philadelphia, PA HCWTM)

Mother Lane was the first missionary sent by Christ Baptist Church, the young Reverend Ben Johnson founder and pastor, Philadelphia, PA.

Mother Lane is a graduate of Manna Bible Institute, Class of 1955. Her first ministry was New Life Boy's Ranch in upstate PA. She was group home mother, housekeeper, and cook. She later went to Sunday Breakfast Association Mission and worked as a cook and ministered to the men at the mission in downtown Philadelphia for many years. In the early 1980s she heard the call from the Lord to go to Nova Scotia, Canada and work as a missionary with a young missionary by the name Debbie Perkins in the South Shore area of Nova Scotia, Canada

Her work in the field of Nova Scotia, Canada and at the headquarters in Philadelphia, PA was over 19 years and is outstanding. At the age of 90, at the time of this writing,

February 11, 2003 Mother Lane still serves at headquarters packing clothes and used eye glasses for our fields in Haiti, West Indies and Liberia West Africa.

One day last year, she packed books from 10:30am - 6:00pm for Africa. Around 8:00p.m. she called headquarters and told me that she had not finished her work and that she would return the next day to complete it. "Don't let anyone touch my work," she said. A woman of her word, she returned the next day and completed the work. Whatsoever thy hands find to do, do it with thy might.

Missionary #67 Julia King, Philadelphia, PA
(Carver Foreign Missions, Atlanta, GA)

Sister King is a member of the Christian Stronghold Baptist Church, Philadelphia, PA, Dr. Willie Richardson, Pastor. She is a graduate of Carver Bible College in Atlanta, GA and is in her third or fourth term of a full-time missionary at Carver Foreign Missions in Painsword, Liberia West Africa. She was sent to Carver Foreign Missions by Have Christ Will Travel Ministries in Dr. Joseph C. Jeter's short term missions program in 1977 for the summer to work with Reverend and Mrs. Donald Canty and a host of missionaries on the mission station there.

She returned to America and completed her Bible education, then did some teaching at a Christian Day School in Kansas City. Judy felt the call to Africa and returned in the mid 1980s. When the war came to Liberia in 1991, Judy returned home to get nursing training and then in late 2000 or 2001 went back to Liberia West Africa.

Her work included teaching at the Carver Mission Academy, mission secretary, teaching Sunday school, Christian Counseling and many other duties.

Judy, as we lovingly call her was a short-term missionary with HCWTM, 1977. Also in 1996 or 1997 she was on loan to our mission again in 1996 or 1997 and worked for 6 months in Nova Scotia, Canada.

Missionary Julia King is an example of a great young dedicated Christian and missionary. Matt 6:33

Missionary #68 Reverend Glenn and Mrs. Kim Mason Philadelphia, PA – Carver Foreign Missions, Atlanta, GA and Liberia West Africa

The Masons are members of Christian Stronghold Baptist Church, Dr. Willie Richardson, Pastor. The Masons are fruit from the ministry of Reverend and Mrs. Donald Canty of Christian Stronghold Baptist Church.

The Masons have two daughters and their entire family was on the field together. Reverend Mason was a Bible teacher at the Monrovia Bible College, Field Leader etc. of Carver Mission. Reverend Glenn Mason is a humble and tender husband, father and leader. Reverend Mason and his family have made many sacrifices in the service of the Lord. They served in Liberia during the war in the mid 1990's and had to be evacuated by helicopter leaving all of their things behind in the mid 1990's.

Reverend Glen Mason was asked by the Carver Mission Leadership Team to become the Director of the Mission in 1999 or 2000. He did except the role and at the time of this writing is still in that job. Preaching, teaching, directing the mission and is assisted by his wife, Kim. Pray much for this young man of God. A giant in Black mission history. St. John 4:35

Reverend Glen Mason was on loan to HCWTM for the summer of 1995. He served in Nova Scotia, Canada. He worked at our camp preaching and teaching the Word of God doing daily vacation Bible School.

Missionary #69 Reverend Harold and Sister June Cottman – (National Baptist Convention of America)

Reverend and Sister Cottman are from the State of New Jersey near the greater Philadelphia area. They left the eastern part of the U.S. and settled in Oakland, C.A.

Desiring to be missionaries, they met the late Reverend Dr. Holley of Mount Zion Missionary Baptist Church, Oakland, CA. Reverend Holley had a great passion for Blacks in foreign missions. He trained the Cottmans in mission work and sent them out as missionaries from that church under the leadership of Dr. J.C. Sams to their mission station in Murryville, Sinoe County, Liberia, W. Africa. Mother Eliza Davis George started this mission station in 1918 when she left Suhem Mission of the National Baptist Convention USA. She walked 200 miles to the town of Greenvillies, Sinoe County.

The work that the Cottmans did was outstanding: they were involved in such work as Christian Education, Church Planting, Evangelism, and other Christian works. The Cottmans were almost forgotten by their Mission Board because of something that happened; I will not discuss at this time. They were discovered by Dr, Joseph C. Jeter in 1970 as he traveled through that remote area of Liberia on his way to visit Mother Maddie Lee Monroe and Mother Eliza Davis George on the Evangelical Negro Industrial Mission deep in the bush in Sinoe County, Liberia, West Africa. Eight years of reports were given to Dr. Joseph C. Jeter. They were taken back to America and hand delivered to Dr. J.C. Sams, President of the National Baptist Convention of America in Shreveport, LA Convocation in September 1970.

The Cottmans did and outstanding job for the Lord among the Krone and Sappo Tribes. They are not known by men, but they are known by God. Where they are at the time of this writing (March 2004) I do not know, but God knows.

Acts 4:11 This is the stone which was set at nought of you builders, which is become the head of the corner. Acts 15:26 Men that have hazarded their lives for the name of our Lord Jesus Christ.

Missionary #70 Emma Lee Haywood, Grand Cain, Louisiana

Emma Lee Haywood was an independent Missionary from Los Angeles, CA. She was a member of the Church of God in Christ in Pasadena, CA. She was an independent missionary to Haiti in the West Indies and she ministered in the Port Au Prince area.

Emma Lee Haywood was born in Grand Cain, Louisiana, June 28, 1926. Missionary Haywood was a member of the Church of God in Christ. In 1975, she went to Port au Prince, Haiti to do orphanage work there. She ministered in Haiti for ten years.

Blessing many children, Missionary Haywood sacrificially led them into saving knowledge of Jesus Christ. Sister Haywood lived by faith and was supported by a group of saints from the greater Los Angeles area.

A group from Mt. Olive Church of God in Christ in Los Angeles supported her efforts. Missionary Haywood served for 10 years in Haiti. She led and cared for many children there. She took care of hundreds of children during her ministry in Haiti. Her health failing she returned to California in 1985. Emma Haywood arrived in Heaven, July 25, 2002.

It is fitting that she be the last missionary in this book. Unknown and yet laboring for souls, living by faith and ministering to children. Thanks be unto God for his unspeakable gift II Corinthians 9:15. Emma Haywood Unknown Soldier.

The End